Fruits of **Sorrow**

Also by Elizabeth V. Spelman

Inessential Woman:
Problems of Exclusion in Feminist Thought

Elizabeth V. Spelman

Fruits of Sorrow

FRAMING OUR ATTENTION TO SUFFERING

Beacon Press

Boston

Beacon Press
25 Beacon Street
Boston, Massachusetts 02108-2892
www.beacon.org

Beacon Press books
are published under the auspices of
the Unitarian Universalist Association of Congregations.

First digital-print edition 2001

Earlier versions of several chapters have appeared elsewhere: chapter 1, in *Feminists Rethink the Self,* ed. Diana Tietjens Meyers (Boulder, Colo.: Westview Press, 1997), 163–176; chapter 2, in *Theory, Power, and Human Emancipation: Dimensions of Radical PHilosophy,* ed. Roger Gottlieb (Philadelphia: Temple University Press, 1993), 221–244; chapter 3, in *Reconstructing Political Theory: Feminist Perspectives,* ed. Mary Lyndon Shanley and Uma Narayan (Oxford: Polity Press, 1997), 128–143; chapter 4, in *Feminist Ethics,* ed. Claudia Card (Lawrence: University Press of Kansas, 1991), 213–232; chapter 5, in *Overcoming Racism and Sexism,* ed. Linda A. Bell and David Blumenfeld (Savage, Md.: Rowman & Littlefield, 1995), 181–196

Library of Congress Cataloging-in-Publication Data
Spelman, Elizabeth V.
Fruits of sorrow : framing our attention to suffering / Elizabeth V. Spelman.
p.   cm.
ISBN 0-8070-1421-4
1. Suffering. I. Title.
B105.S79S68   1997
128´.4—dc21   96-53179

For Roo

Contents

Acknowledgments

Surely there is a commandment somewhere according to which a book with "suffering" in its title shall not inflict unecessary pain on the reader. Whatever success this work has in hewing to such a rule is due to the careful criticism, generous suggestions, and timely support of many people. For help on various parts of this book, I am very grateful to Kathy Addelson, Ernie Alleva, Linda Bell, Larry Blum, David Blumenfeld, Richmond Campbell, Sue Campbell, Claudia Card, Betsy Clark, Frances Smith Foster, Sarah Franklin, Margit Franz, Roger Gottlieb, Ken Greenberg, Donna Gunn, Pamela Hall, Alice Hearst, Teresia Hinga, Reni Hofmueller, Barbara Houston, Carolyn Jacobs, Liz Lerman, Susan Levin, Helen Longino, Deborah Lubar, Diana Tietjens Meyers, Field Mithoefer, Kate Morgan, Herta Nagel, Uma Narayan, Dorothy Smith Patterson, Ranu Samantrai, Susan Sherwin, Joe Singer, Joanna Slater, Jon Spelman, the late Tom Tymoczko, and Deborah Wolf. I especially thank Nalini Bhushan, Martha Minow, Molly Shanley, and Ruth Solie for the extraordinary expression of friendship and collegiality in painstakingly scrutinizing the entire manuscript. Kathryn Blatt's copyediting was as friendly as it was scrupulous. Lauren

Acknowledgments

Bryant's advice in the early phases of my thinking about the scope of the book and Andy Hrycyna's enthusiastic and inspired editorial guidance on the road to its completion have reminded me of my good fortune in working once again with Beacon Press.

For abetting this project by underwriting residencies at their institutions, I am happily indebted to Connie Buchanan and the Harvard Divinity School, and to Cornelia Klinger and the Institut für die Wissenschaften vom Menschen in Vienna. For the many blessings of their ongoing companionship, affectionate thanks to my colleagues and students at Smith College.

Fruits of **Sorrow**

SUFFERING AND
THE ECONOMY OF ATTENTION

*G*iven *the ubiquity of suffering,* and its complex claims upon our attention, organizing such attention would seem to be both a psychological and a social necessity. As we sift through and try to make sense of the suffering to which we are called on to respond, we implicitly and explicitly sort out, measure, and give shape to it. Some ways of focusing on and framing suffering seem particularly well geared to affirming the dignity and humanity of sufferers even as their experiences threaten to crush or diminish them. Among these forms of attention are three familiar and historically significant portrayals of sufferers: as the subjects of tragedy; as the objects of compassion; and as spiritual bellhops,[1] carriers of experience from which others can benefit. I suggest in this book that as welcome as these responses often are, there is much about the ways in which they distribute attention to suffering that makes them morally and politically problematic.

This then is not a book about the nature of suffering. I take examples from but do not closely examine specific experiences falling under the rubric of human suffering, such as torture, genocide, slavery, starvation, oppression, exploitation, destitution, disease, death, grief, and physical and mental cruelty. Nor do I offer advice or instruction about how to come to grips with such suffering, individually or through political mobilization. Clumsy and unfriendly as such disclaimers always are, in this case their absence would be disingenuous. Precisely because thoughtful treatments of the nature of suffering, and useful guides to dealing with it, promise timely changes in people's lives, it is important to make clear right away that this book fits into neither category.

In this connection what follows is concerned not with what experts have to say about suffering, but with what *we* say about sufferers and the meaning of their suffering as we employ familiar and everyday ways of responding to people in pain. Indeed, whether or not it is our lot as humans to suffer, it often seems as if it is our lot to attempt to give form to suffering—be it our own, that of those close to us, or that of strangers near and far.

A brief and partial catalog of the variety of ways we are involved in trying to make sense of suffering can help locate the three specific shapes of attention to suffering that will occupy us.

First of all, our lives are littered with judgments about suffering: whether someone is suffering, how much someone hurts, how much attention her suffering should get, how much attention one can give without suffering too much oneself, whose suffering should get attention first, whose suffering might be good for them, whose suffering isn't as bad as they think, who deserves to suffer, who doesn't.[2] In the case of denizens of late-twentieth-century Western nations, judgments of this sort show up every day, in the advice we offer friends about how to deal with dying relatives, in the opinions we have about welfare, in our nods of agreement or protests of disagreement with the punishments given to torturers or rapists, in the way we decide to parcel out our attention to the daily onslaught of news about atrocities around the world and in our own backyards.

Perhaps in hopes that making suffering intelligible will make it bearable, maybe even controllable, we call on our prodigious capacities as taxonomists and as wielders of distinctions. We can start with a small sample of familiar if not universally agreed-upon ways that we enlist our distinction-making abilities in the service of trying to make sense of what we suffer. Sometimes we distinguish kinds of suffering by reference to their causes, perhaps among other reasons because it matters to us whether human agency is involved. Thus it appears that some suffering is our lot simply because we are flesh-and-blood creatures, fragile, mortal, and not in control of nature. Other suffering seems more immediately traceable to the intentions of our fellow humans to harm us. On some occasions we may think of it as the unintended byproduct of someone else's pursuit of happiness, or for that matter of our own.

Sometimes we distinguish among kinds of suffering, perhaps in connection with attempts to rank instances of suffering by degree of severity, perhaps in the process of trying to figure out how to put an end to the suffering in question (or, alas, to bring it about). For example, those of us drawn to Cartesian tidiness may be tempted to tote up our sufferings under two columns, one labeled "mental" and one labeled "physical"—though Descartes himself seemed to find this distinction confounded in the case of everyday pain.[3]

Among our attempts to make sense of human suffering is the somewhat paradoxical distinction between suffering of which we can make sense and suffering of which we cannot. Do some forms of suffering mark a place in human life where the desire to make one's experience intelligible to others, perhaps even to oneself, cannot be satisfied? Is it the case, as Elaine Scarry has argued, that physical pain is fundamentally unsharable, and only with great effort becomes part of the intersubjective commerce of language?[4]

Accompanying the concern that there may be forms of suffering too submerged in the dumb recesses of the human body ever to find articulation in human speech is what appears to be the opposite worry: that once rendered intelligible through its articulation in language or its representability in art, suffering becomes ready for use and thus also for possible abuse by others. The expression of our pain or suffering that makes it available to others opens up the possibility that they will understand what it means to us, but also the possibility that others will mangle our account, especially if they stretch, tuck, or hem our experience in an attempt to tailor it to make sense of their own.

Such questions lead to the final entry in this small sample of means by which we distinction-wielding humans try to manage our suffering, at least conceptually. We find ourselves, whether we really want to or not, comparing and contrasting different instances of suffering, and assigning relative weights to them. There is no one without suffering in their own lives, in the lives of those for whom they care, and in the local and not-so-local worlds in which they live. In response to their own and others' suffering, individuals and communities husband and distribute their emotional and economic resources in quite particular ways. Some suffering commands our attention forcefully; some of it we judge not to be our business, or maybe not deserving of our concern, or perhaps not demanding as strong a response as the suffering of those closer to home.

In this book I describe forms in which such economy of attention is shaped. In particular I scrutinize three responses that serve to bring attention to the suffering of some people but not others as noteworthy, deserving of our concern, or instructive for us as human beings.

Sufferers as the subjects of tragedy. Referring to suffering as tragic, or to sufferers as tragic figures, is a common and very old way of giving weight to the meaning of a particular experience of suffering or to the significance of a particular person's suffering. While there are not any simple or transhistorical criteria for what constitutes tragic suffering,[5] what appears to remain constant about the concept of the tragic is that it operates rhetorically to arrest attention, to signal that the suffering being taken note of is—or ought to be—especially gripping or instructive or worthy of more than cursory recognition. While I do not examine the history of the idea of the tragic, I begin by recognizing the fact that the earliest history of Western philosophy is marked by a struggle between the claims of tragic theater and the claims of philosophical inquiry. Chapter 1 explores Plato's anxiety about the seductive pull of grief that he thought central to the tragic theater. Teaching in the *Republic* that philosopher-kings and philosopher-queens must get grief right, must know when, why, and how to grieve, Plato hoped to limit grief in the face of human suffering, indeed, to greatly reduce the kind of suffering to which grief seems such a natural response.

One of the ways Aristotle marked out his distance from Plato was in finding a place for grief, even for cultivating it. But not just any grief. Aristotle's *Poetics* tells us whose suffering is grievous enough to deserve our attention, whose suffering is instructive enough that we learn something from it. If we juxtapose Aristotle's famous views about tragedy with his equally influential and infamous views about those who are slaves "by nature," it becomes clear that an Aristotelian slave could never be the subject of an Aristotelian tragedy. Precisely because referring to suffering as tragic highlights some suffering as more deserving of our attention than other kinds, it is worth exploring whose suffering comes to be regarded as tragic and whose does not. In chapter 2 I employ Aristotelian themes to argue that understanding American slavery as "the American tragedy" gives short shrift to the suffering of African American slaves.

Sufferers as the objects of compassion. If the idea of the tragic is a common means by which our attention is directed to suffering, the injunction to feel compassion is a familiar way in which we are encouraged to respond to the sufferers who have our attention. For example, readers of Harriet A. Jacobs's *Incidents in the Life of a Slave Girl* probably are not surprised that Jacobs, who had been a slave, would appeal to the compassion of people she had reason to believe regarded such feeling for the subjugated as a virtue, perhaps even as a duty: white Christian women of the northern United States.

6

However, Jacobs also was acutely attuned to the political and psychological risks sometimes entailed in becoming the object of compassion. On the one hand, compassion tends to organize the resources of the compassionate person in a way that can be enormously consoling and practically helpful to the sufferer. But compassion, like other forms of caring, may also reinforce the very patterns of economic and political subordination responsible for such suffering. Thus Jacobs was aware of the strong possibility that white northern women's compassion for Black slaves would constitute a reiteration of rather than resistance to long-entrenched patterns of white-Black relations under slavery. In chapter 3 I juxtapose Jacobs's worries about compassion to those of Hannah Arendt, who, like Jacobs, mightily distrusted public professions of compassion, but who was much less keen than Jacobs appeared to be about political struggles over the meaning of an individual's or a group's experience of suffering.

The fact that Jacobs appeals especially to northern white *women* reminds us that the economy of attention to suffering has several dimensions. While such an economy works to focus concern for some kinds of suffering and not others, it also may enlist or conscribe some people but not others to pay the requisite attention. That is, there is likely to be a division of labor in the organization of attention to suffering. The assumption that women are to do the work of caring has been under severe scrutiny by feminists. The publication of Carol Gilligan's *In a Different Voice* and Nel Noddings's *Caring* launched vigorous and ongoing debate over the meaning and implications of the idea that women are much more likely than men to be guided by an "ethic of care" in their understanding and response to moral quandaries. I don't join in that debate, but in chapter 4 I highlight what I take to be obscured or ignored by it: the history of women's cruelty to one another, and the ways in which the muting of that history, even in a cautious and qualified celebration of women's careful attending to the needs of others, threatens to blind us to uncomfortable moral facts. For instance, Jacobs's reliance on a plea for the compassion of some women occurs in the context of her fully expecting the cruel ministrations and daily humiliations of others.

Sufferers as "spiritual bellhops," carriers of experience from which others can benefit. A theme only adumbrated in earlier chapters is taken up in fuller force in chapter 5: is suffering an equalizer—does humans' shared vulnerability to suffering mean that we are likely to find common ground in the fact of our suffering? Or is it the case that because none of us is ever fully indemnified against suffering, we invent so many ways to make suffering tell *against* the recognition that we all have friable souls and pokable bodies? To ask this is not to ignore the fact that some people are much better insured against suffering than others—such unequal protection is a large part of what it means to have or not have access to the economic, political, and psychological resources of the family, the community, the nation, the globe. It is, however, to wonder aloud about whether human suffering is one of those places where some humans have gone to some length to mark differences among people precisely because our relatively equal capacity for suffering threatens to demand acknowledgment of equality in other areas.[6] If Aristotle thought all people suffer, but some suffer in more interesting and instructive ways than others, some nineteenth-century apologists for slavery in the United States argued that Blacks were just less susceptible to physical pain and emotional bereavement than whites.[7] That is one of the reasons why, when Harriet Jacobs asked white northern women to think about what it meant to be separated from their own children as a means of coming to understand the horrors of slavery, she was making an end run around one of the tenets of white racial supremacist thought.

And yet claims of shared human suffering can do as much to reinforce claims of superiority and inferiority as they can to undermine them. It depends on how the claims are made, who makes them, and to what end. This becomes particularly clear when one person or group attempts to borrow the experience of another person or group to make sense of their own suffering.

For example, some white women living in the mid-nineteenth-century United States tried to bring attention to their economic, social, and political plight by referring to themselves as slaves. This was not surprising: many of them were or had been abolitionists, and they aimed their appeal in part at abolitionist audiences. Moreover, this was hardly the first or the last time in human history that one group likened the nature and severity and significance of its suffering to that of the already recognized and canonized suffering of others: a familiar late-twentieth-century example is the broad characterization of the AIDS epidemic as another Holocaust.

But such equations or conflations or borrowings raise vexing moral and political issues—notoriously so. On the one hand, the use of one's suffering by others appears to offer at least partial redemption for that suffering: what I or what we went through might turn out to be of help to others; if so, my experiences are not anomalous or at the margins of human existence, but representative of or paradigmatic for the rest of humankind. To the degree that those inflicting suffering try to justify their acts on the grounds that the sufferers are not fully human, the honor apparently paid to such suffering by its being treated as exemplary may signal an important acknowledgment of shared human status. But the very articulation of this possibility also invites close scrutiny: what if the borrowers are in fact more like scavengers, interested in the suffering of others not as a way of marking deep and pervasive similarities among suffering humanity, and making a case for mutual care, but mainly as a way of trying to garner concern simply for themselves? When are they honoring the suffering of others, when simply compounding it by expropriating yet another product of the horrific labors of the sufferers—their now "exemplary" experiences of suffering?

The representations by means of which we can learn about suffering, or learn from it, simultaneously provide occasions for the commodification of suffering, avenues for the traffic in sorrow and grief. This is perhaps most clear in the case of commercial advertisements that employ stark or muted images of suffering in order to win the attention and the approval of potential buyers. Some ads—the notorious Benetton pictures of impoverished children—are carefully calculated to get viewers and consumers to strongly associate feeling good about their caring response to suffering with the pleasures of purchase and ownership. People who buy and wear a certain brand of clothing are people with compassion for the oppressed. Other ads suggest not so much that people who buy and wear certain clothes care for suffering humanity but rather that they are part of suffering humanity, as in the Calvin Klein ad which more or less tells us that men who wear blue jeans are part of the family of men who dug the subway tunnels of Manhattan.

But what is obvious in the crasser corners of advertising— the use of images of suffering for the sake not of the sufferer but the presenter or the viewer—takes on a less obvious form in the world of art. If critics of advertising worry about the use of representations of suffering for the commercial enrichment of their purveyors, some art critics worry about the use of such representations for the aesthetic delectation of the viewer. The latter is in fact part of a cluster of concerns about the right distance for a work of art to strike between itself and the suffering it portrays. Too far, so one kind of worry goes, and the suffering of some becomes simply the occasion for the lovely aesthetic experience of others; but too close, so another kind goes, and there is really not any art at all, but simply barely mediated suffering. The surfacing of this latter concern in a highly provocative piece of dance criticism provides the occasion for chapter 6. The eminent dance critic Arlene Croce announced her refusal to attend a performance on the grounds that, confident ahead of time that the event was going to consist mostly of the parading of people suffering from AIDS and other terminal illnesses, there was nothing for her to do as a critic; the proper response to actual suffering is to feel compassion (though, as we shall see, Croce herself seems also to have felt contempt), not to stand back and critically assess the sufferers. Croce turns out to echo some of Plato's anxieties about the moral and political dangers facing what they both take to be unwary and insufficiently vigilant audiences exposed to representations of suffering in the theater. Like Plato, she insists that how we engage with the suffering humanity around us affects and mirrors the health of our souls and the health of the society.

By placing the chapters focusing on Plato and Croce at the beginning and end, I suggest that art often mediates our relation to suffering. Not all art does that, of course; but one of the prominent functions of theater, literature, painting, and dance[8] is to get us to think and feel in particular ways about particular kinds and instances of suffering—tragic heros or heroines, persecuted saviors, exhausted laborers, the diseased and the dying. It is not a big step from thinking about how these obvious examples from art arrest, frame, and focus our attention on suffering to considering the many other means there are by which our relation to suffering is mediated.

Indeed the variety and ubiquity of such means are exemplified in what may appear to be the rather motley collection of authors and topics covered in these pages. It is perhaps already clear, especially to those readers adept at reading intellectual droppings, that this is the work of someone in conversation with—though not necessarily in agreement with—figures from several recognizable and overlapping areas of inquiry: nineteenth- and twentieth-century African American social and political thought; late-twentieth-century North American feminist theory; the history of Western philosophy.

With respect to this last-mentioned resource, contemporary readers of academic philosophical journals and books may be forgiven for having the impression that what are called professional philosophers have left examination of human suffering to other inquirers. A typical volume of *The Philosopher's Index* has few entries under the subject topic "suffering," and most of them direct readers to articles in journals of biomedicine or theology. *The Encyclopedia of Philosophy* does not have an entry for suffering, though the index refers the persistent inquirer to entries on Freud and Reinhold Niebuhr, figures whom academic philosophers might use as pinch hitters but never think of as Hall of Famers. With few exceptions Anglo-American philosophers seem to have gone out of their way not to contribute to discussions about, for example, U.S. slavery or the Holocaust, as if these somehow are better left to historians, theologians, or literary critics.[9]

Perhaps this is simply a matter of how problems in philosophy today are cataloged or marked for access; perhaps it has to do with the predilection for taking tiny conceptual gardens and cultivating them to the hilt rather than posing the "big questions" for humanity that nonphilosophers at least sometimes expect philosophers to address. In any event, this book is not the place for trying to turn these patently cursory observations into a persuasive argument about the relative absence of attention to suffering in the Anglo-American version of "real philosophy," or the probable causes and possible significance of that absence. I present this very rough sketch of how an influential segment of contemporary professional philosophy understands its proper jurisdiction in order to highlight, by way of contrast, Plato's sense of the provenance of philosophy. The author of the *Republic* explicitly suggests that philosophy has something crucial to say about human suffering.[10] Far from abdicating responsibility to historians or theologians or anyone else for how to think about suffering, Plato was intent on wresting authority in such matters from poets and others he regarded as dangerously ill-informed sources whom Athenians depended on for understanding the origin and the meaning of what grieved them.

Plato receives a close reading in the first chapter. In taking an apparently shocking position about the proper attitude toward suffering, he sets an illuminating conceptual, historical, and political context for the chapters that follow. Let us see, then, why Plato thought it so important to get grief right.

GOOD GRIEF! IT'S PLATO!

*T*here is a superficial sense in which Plato, who casts such a long shadow on the way we in the West have thought about ourselves, seems not to have been concerned about human suffering. His work was in many ways an attempt to dislodge Homer and the tragic poets—suffering mavens if ever there were—as the educators of Athenians. But he did not try to tell new stories about the old heroes and heroines. He appears, on the contrary, to have tried to get rid of the stories altogether. For example, however successful his principal character Socrates was as a soldier, his struggles and conquests on the battlefield are not the focus of Plato's interest. Whatever Socrates' family life was like, he is not known to us because he slept with his mother or gobbled up his children. Socrates is not portrayed as a tragic figure—at the very least, we certainly do not get the idea from Plato that we, any more than his wife, Xanthippe,[1] ought to grieve profusely over Socrates' being misunderstood by others, his trial, or his death. His demise, unjust though it may seem to us, is presented in such a way that we are not supposed to be greatly pained by it, nor to take bittersweet pleasure in the pain.

Indeed, when it comes to grief, Plato appears to have been the spoilsport of fourth-century Athens. He seems to have drawn the curtain in front of the grand dramas of human suffering, those almost morbidly seductive tales about human misery and the human species' indefatigable attempts to make it intelligible. Readers of the *Republic* are meant to learn that tantalizing spectacles of humans sabotaging themselves or doing in their loved ones are bound to trigger grief, for which there is little place in the well-ordered soul and the well-ordered state.

But the fact that he does not dwell on suffering, nor leave us with his own cast of tragic figures, hardly means Plato was not occupied, even preoccupied, with human misery. This is particularly clear in the *Republic*, in which Socrates not only goes after the tragic poets but also the cynical Thrasymachus for their failure to understand the proper place of grief. The dialogue provides a blueprint for the elimination, or at least the mitigation, of the evils to which humans are subject; it both specifies the political conditions under which such evils would not arise, and articulates beliefs about the proper weight to give such evils should we be confronted with them. If we come to comprehend all this, Plato suggests, perhaps we cannot eliminate grief but get it right, even though Homer and the tragic poets could not.

A word about terminology. Plato, as we shall see, wants us

to understand the proper place of grief in individual and collective life, but he also wants us to acquire correct beliefs about the nature and meaning of pain, pleasure, and happiness. In the *Republic* all this happens in the context of a lengthy exploration of justice. Plato did not, and we should not, treat "grief" and "suffering" and "pain" and "unhappiness" as synonyms.[2] As will be clear from the context, sometimes the topic under discussion is grief in particular, that is, intensely felt anguish over the death of loved ones, or, at its outer edges, suffering suffused with the sense of irreparable loss. But sometimes the discussion covers other forms of physical and psychological suffering more broadly, and other times—most generally of all—a sense of unhappiness.

TRAGEDY AND
THE MISUNDERSTANDING OF GRIEF

According to Plato, when you get grief wrong you get much else wrong too. Homer and the tragedians were dangerously wrong about grief and about how to assess the events to which it is a response. They come under Socratic scrutiny as creators (among other things) of mimetic poetry.[3] Such poetry is defined in book 10 of the *Republic* as that which "imitates human beings acting under compulsion or voluntarily, and as a result of their actions supposing themselves to have fared well or ill and in all this feeling either grief or joy" (603c). Whether or not Plato had Oedipus in mind when proffering this definition, he can be invoked in order to illustrate what appears to be Plato's point: *Oedipus Rex* enacts the story of a man, apparently acting voluntarily, who unwittingly kills his father and marries his mother; though for some time he assumes he has fared well, he comes to see what in fact he has done, and, realizing the great ills that have befallen him and his family and his city, he becomes sorely grieved. Tragic heroes typically are presented as being driven in their grief to lamentation and breast-beating (605d). Oedipus, of course, goes a bit further and gouges out his eyes.

Plato is worried about the powerful, complicated effects such portrayals of grief have on their audiences. On the one hand, he says, audiences tend to react with pleasure: we "feel pleasure, and abandon ourselves and accompany the representation [of suffering and grief] with sympathy and eagerness, and we praise as an excellent poet the one who most strongly affects us in this way" (605d). The pleasure presumably is due to the audience's delight not in what the hero finds grievous but in the feeling of sympathy for the aggrieved hero and in the ability of the poet to affect the audience so powerfully.[4]

This pleasure seems to presuppose a kind of distance between the hero and the member of the audience: the hero is suffering greatly but the audience is filled with delight. At the same time—and this is why the effects of mimetic poetry are so complex—what Plato finds disturbing about the power of such poetry is that the pleasure produced in the members of the audience strengthens their willingness to yield to their own grief. The pleasure they take in the representation of the pain of another strengthens the part of them that would grieve for themselves. This "plaintive part" of the soul by its very nature hungers for "tears and a good cry and satisfaction" (606a); it shamelessly praises and pities "another who, claiming to be a good man, abandons himself to excess in his grief" (606b). If we take pleasure in seeing another grieve, then we will not restrain our own grief, for we will take pleasure also in our own grieving: "For after feeding fat the emotion of pity there, it is not easy to restrain it in our own sufferings" (606b). Such pleasure in our own grieving is dangerous, Plato insists, because the heaving grieving we praise in the theater is "that of a woman"; it is unbecoming for noble men to allow themselves to give in to such grief. It undermines their capacity to "remain calm and endure" when "affliction comes" in their real lives (605 d–e; cf. 395e).

In short, the great tragic scenes make grief seductive—even for those who know better—by highlighting and underscoring the pleasures of grief. Members of the audience presumably are not pleased by the sufferings of the hero, but they are pleased by the chance to satisfy their desire to wail and shed tears. Mimetic poets know all too well how to appeal to the part of us that grieves, "that leads us to dwell in memory on our suffering and impels us to lamentation, and cannot get enough of that sort of thing . . . the irrational and idle part of us, the associate of cowardice" (604d).

Mimetic poets are dangerous because they strengthen the power of this irrational part of the soul over the rational. That with which we grieve is at odds with the "nobly serious part" (603c), in virtue of which one follows "reason and law" (604a–b). (In terms of the *Republic's* tripartite division of the soul into reason, spirit, and appetite [439a ff.], the emotion of grief seems to be located in the spirit, which is capable of serving the rational element by reining in the unruly forces belonging to the appetite. But Socrates' references to the voraciousness and insatiability of grief also implicitly liken it to a kind of appetite that knows no limits.)[5]

A "good and reasonable man" can't help but feel pain when in his own life something horrible happens, such as the death of a son. But he will be "moderate in his grief" (603e), for reason tells him that "it is best to keep quiet as far as possible in calamity and not to chafe and repine, because we cannot know what is really good and evil in such things and it advantages us nothing to take them hard, and nothing in mortal life is worthy of great concern, and our grieving checks the very thing we need to come to our aid as quickly as possible in such case" (604c).[6] One needs to think through what has happened and what one ought to do, rather than "clapping one's hands to the stricken spot and wasting the time in wailing"; one should "accustom the soul to devote itself at once to the curing of the hurt and the raising up of what has fallen" (604d). Grieving makes our condition worse, because it distracts us from attending thoughtfully to the situation we find so grievous.[7] We put off or sabotage what we really should be doing when faced with the loss of loved ones, the injustice of others, the difficult infirmities of life, the bony certainty of death: try to cure what can be cured, try to put together what has been rent asunder, try to be brave, fearless, resolute.

Homer and the tragedians are masterful in rendering the pleasures and pains of their characters, and they know how to create pleasure and bittersweet pain in their audiences. But they know next to nothing about the proper role of pleasure and pain in human life. More specifically, they don't know how to take the proper measure of grief.

Moreover, in their explanations of the role of the gods, the poets put forth dangerously misleading ideas about the cause of human misery more generally. They say that "the gods themselves assign to many good men misfortunes and an evil life, but to their opposites a contrary lot" (364b); and that the gods can be bought off by evil men, who then will not have to pay for their wrongdoing (364d–e). In short, "if we are to believe [the poets], the thing to do is to commit injustice and offer sacrifice from the fruits of our wrongdoing. For if we are just, we shall, it is true, be unscathed by the gods, but we shall be putting away from us the profits of injustice, but if we are unjust, we shall win those profits, and, by the importunity of our prayers, when we transgress and sin we shall persuade them and escape scot free" (365e–366a).

Such views, Plato insists, are deeply and insidiously wrong. Although the gods are responsible for what is good, they are not responsible for what is evil (379c). It is imperative for humans not to think the gods are the cause of evil: "every man will be very lenient with his own misdeeds if he is convinced" that gods do dreadful things to other gods or to humans (391e, 619c).

In sum, there are many reasons why, according to Plato, we should be careful not to be beguiled by the scenes of grief so poignantly rendered by Homer and the tragedians. The poets seriously mislead us about the source of human misery. Their powerful representations of suffering and anguish stir up our insatiable appetite-like desire for experiencing grief, thereby subverting reason and causing us to fail to pay proper attention to what we ought to do. In contemporary terms, the poets' treatment of grief misleads us theologically, ethically, and epistemologically.

THRASYMACHUS AND
THE INDIVIDUATION OF GRIEF

One reason mimetic poets are so dangerous, Plato insists, is that they provide powerful dramatic "examples of men who, though unjust, are happy, and of just men who are wretched" (392b). In so doing the poets join forces with Thrasymachus, the blustery *provocateur* of book 1 of the *Republic*, to whose views about justice the rest of the dialogue is a response.

According to Thrasymachus, "the most consummate form of injustice ... makes the man who has done the wrong most happy," whereas "those who are wronged and who would not themselves willingly do wrong [are] most miserable" (344a). Socrates appears to persuade him to change his mind. But as book 2 opens, Socrates' young friends Glaucon and Adimantus desperately appeal to him to respond at greater length to Thrasymachus because, they insist, much of the culture around them affirms Thrasymachus' view that any fool knows it is better to be unjust than to be just. From Thrasymachus and "innumerable others" (358d), young men hear that though the reputation for justice brings rewards, justice itself is an "affliction" (358a).

The Thrasymachus-inspired case for the wretchedness of the just man, and the happiness of the unjust, is this: the just man does not satisfy his natural desires to take as much as he can from everyone else around him. Given that these desires are natural for others to have about our possessions, it not only cannot benefit us to be just, but our being just will benefit those who act unjustly. By the very nature of their desires, other men will "do wrong" to us. They will take our possessions, steal our wives (women do not appear in Thrasymachus' discussion except as the objects of male desire), kill us if they please, and enslave us if they can get away with it (360b–c). Justice, on this view, arises in order to mitigate the starkness of these options: it is a "compromise between the best, which is to do wrong with impunity, and the worst, which is to be wronged and be impotent to get one's revenge" (359a). So we might agree to be just, but only because we figure that even if this means our desires for the possessions of others cannot be satisfied, at least other people's desires for our house and wife and life cannot be satisfied either.

Thrasymachus seems to assume that the desires which it is so natural to want to satisfy are desires for things the possession of which necessarily will involve frustrating the desires of others. More simply, the view is that our happiness requires the misery of others, and their happiness requires that we be wretched. Satisfying our desires means leaving other people's desires thwarted; we either do harm to others or have it done to us.

Socrates thinks Thrasymachus is mistaken from head to foot, that he is mistaken about human nature, about the nature of justice, and about the meaning of happiness and misery. For our purposes, a crucial difference between Thrasymachus and Socrates turns on the possibility of seeing our happiness as compatible with the happiness of others, and of seeing other people's misery as affecting the possibility of our own.

Thrasymachus seems to see happiness as a zero-sum game: if I am happy, I must be doing something that is making someone else unhappy, since the desires I need to satisfy in order to be happy are desires for what belongs to someone else and would make them unhappy to be without. But according to Socrates, the happiest person is the just person, and the just person is one in whom each part of the soul is playing its appropriate role. When reason—if not our own, then someone else's—is master of the appetites, the happiness of one person is fully compatible with the happiness of another.[8]

Implied in Thrasymachus' views about happiness and misery is the assumption that the misery of other people doesn't touch us. Yet, although other people's misery is not itself the object of our desires, it is the necessary byproduct of our desires being satisfied. The misery of other people is the necessary consequence of our being happy, but it is of no direct concern to us—except insofar as their own unsatisfied desires make them prey on us. We are interested in what brings pleasure to us, not in what brings pleasure or pain to anyone else.

For Socrates, how people think about the relation between their own and other people's suffering is directly connected to how well run a state is and how its citizens fare. The greatest evil for a state is whatever "makes it many instead of one" (462b). Citizens cannot be bound together and act as one body when "some grieve exceedingly and others rejoice at the same happenings" (462b–c). Crucial to the existence of a unitary, unfragmented community, then, is a "community of pleasure and pain," which we can observe when "all the citizens rejoice and grieve alike" at the same things (462b); when, "as far as practicable," there is "one experience of pleasure and pain" (464d).

Whether a community has shared or individual experiences of grief and joy depends on the extent to which that community allows individual ownership of property. Some of the most famous, or infamous, passages from book 5 of the *Republic* are those in which Plato presents arguments against the private ownership of property, whether in the form of material objects or human beings. One sure source of fragmentation and dissension among people is the possibility of men referring to things as "mine" rather than "ours," "one man dragging off to his own house anything he is able to acquire apart from the rest, and another doing the same to his own separate house, and having women and children apart" (464d). On the other hand, if they "have nothing in private possession but their bodies, but all else in common . . . we can count on their being free from the dissensions that arise among men from the possession of property, children, and kin" (464e). In short, in this view it is individual ownership that "introduc[es] into the state the pleasures and pains of individuals" (464d). Individualization of pleasure and pain, a grave threat to the unity of the state, is due to individualization of property.

Thrasymachus assumed that as a matter of course men (again, women are objects and not subjects of desire for him) distinguish their own pleasures and pains from the pleasures and pains of others, and seek to pursue what brings them pleasure at the expense of bringing pain to others. But Socrates insists that it is not a given, as Thrasymachus assumes, that we will take pleasure in performing actions that we know to cause great misery in others. We can learn to take pleasure in what pleases other people; we can learn to grieve at what gives them pain; indeed, we can come to be pained by and be pleased by the same things they do. People will grieve over misfortunes they count as theirs, and rejoice in good things they do or that happen to them. But what they count as "theirs" or "not theirs" depends on the kind of polity in which they live.

In sum, Thrasymachus gets grief wrong no less than the poets did. He badly misunderstands its place in human life. He imagines that we can't help but grieve if our desires are not satisfied—not only because it is natural to want to satisfy our desires, and thus presumably to feel great loss when they are thwarted, but also because the only conceivable cause of not satisfying our desires is that another person is satisfying his, necessarily at our expense. Indeed, Thrasymachus doesn't understand the plasticity of our desire, so he can't imagine the possibility that rather than one person's happiness necessarily being paired with another's misery, people can suffer over and rejoice in the same thing.

Audiences bewitched by the power of poets are all too liable to have their own capacity for debilitating grief kindled by beholding the grief of others. But young men bewitched by the rhetorical powers of a Thrasymachus are equally liable to think that other people's suffering has no hold on them at all. We should learn from the criticism of the poets that succumbing to grief is conduct unbecoming those whose capacity for reason qualifies, indeed obliges, them to rule and thus to do their part in maintaining unity and order in the state. But at the same time we are to learn from the attack on the moral and psychological blindness of Thrasymachus that another great principle of unity in the state is the capacity of all to rejoice and mourn over the same events.

THE POETS, THRASYMACHUS, AND SOCRATES

For the mimetic poets, tragedy seems not only to allow but to require that those who are most just are also the most wretched. This view about the inverse relation between justice and misery is heartily endorsed by Thrasymachus. But notice how differently the poets and Thrasymachus—at least as we see them through the eyes of Plato—portray grief and other forms of misery.

The tragedians are said to make getting caught up in the grief of another a pleasurable experience and in our own grief allowable, even seductive. But Thrasymachus never talks about suffering in a way that makes experiencing it, even vicariously, seem at all attractive. On the contrary, Thrasymachus implies that people in a position to grieve about their lot are at best pitiable weaklings who have bought a bill of goods about the importance of being just and instead end up the most wretched of humans. There is nothing great about their suffering; it has nothing to teach them, or those who observe them, except the lesson that the happiest people are those who are unjust.

Thus, according to the *Republic*, the tragedians teach that justice is perhaps worth striving for but often leaves one grieving or dead, while Thrasymachus insists that justice is not worth striving for precisely because it will lead to grief over the loss of what one naturally desires. From Socrates we get the idea that justice is worth striving for and not only will not leave one in grief but in fact brings one happiness properly understood. Close examination of these strong differences between Socrates and his opponents reveals some surprising points of contact.

First, dead set as he is on countering Thrasymachus' views, Socrates is closer to him than he is to the tragedians (as Socrates interprets them) in deflecting the gravitational pull of grief. Socrates shares Thrasymachus' strong aversion to situations that we know will bring us grief and other kinds of pain. Just as one of the reasons Socrates offers for not giving in to grief is that it diverts our attention from responding appropriately to the situation that brings such suffering, so according to Thrasymachus the smart and happy man will vigilantly avoid relationships with other people that are likely to bring misery of any sort to him. For Thrasymachus the smart and happy man will not subscribe to "justice" precisely because that would require him to lose, or even never to gain, at least some of what is most desirable to him. Socrates and Thrasymachus disagree radically about whether justice or injustice leads to happiness, but they share the impulse to live by standards that counsel the avoidance of grief.

Second, it looks as if Socrates' view about the posssibilty and desirability of grief being shared rather than individualized puts him in a position closer to the mimetic poets than he might be willing to acknowledge. As we have seen, part of Socrates' reply to a Thrasymachus-inspired view is that occasions for grief not only can but should be shared if a community is to have any hopes of unity. But how is this "community of pleasure and pain" (462b) different from what Socrates himself says happens at the theater? Isn't what is problematic about the mimetic poets precisely that they are so adept at creating communities of pleasure and pain in the audience? How can tragedy be so dangerous if it affects large groups of people in such a way that they jointly rejoice in the success of the hero and jointly wail at his demise?

The Platonic response seems to go something like this: Yes, the unity of a community depends on all the members of the community grieving and rejoicing over the same things. In that sense there appears to be some place for grief in the best city. However, the community must grieve and rejoice in the right way over the right things.

But how, according to Plato, can members of the polis arrive at this stage? How can they get grief right?

GOOD GRIEF

It is one thing to give an account of how the poets and Thrasymachus get grief wrong. It is quite another to prescribe the psychological, social, and political conditions under which people might come to grieve in the appropriate manner. Several of the conditions Plato specifies in this connection are closely connected to his views about the proper role of women in the polis and the proper understanding of feminine and masculine traits in the philosopher-rulers.

When we grieve over what happens to great heroes and their families and cities, and are tempted to conclude that suffering is endemic to human life, we fail to ask whether the kinds of social and political conditions under which they lived nourished the very conditions which ultimately led to such suffering and grief.[9] For example, battles among men over the ownership of women often are implicated in the grave tragic situations that the poets present in such dangerously powerful ways. But if the *Republic*'s proposals about family life were to be adopted, no man would own any particular woman, so his own wife could not be taken away from him. This would considerably reduce the kind of occasions for mad jealousy such as those that led to the Trojan War; at the very least, Menelaus could not have complained that Paris kidnapped his wife. Moreover, if any child from a given generation is to be considered any woman's child, any future Jocasta would have to assume that a younger man is her child.

Plato also suggests that there might be less grieving if people could develop a sense of shame at giving in to grief. Socrates tries to induce such shame by characterizing the readiness to grieve as the behavior of a woman.[10] Although Plato appears to argue in book 5 of the *Republic* that women as well as men would be among the philosopher-rulers, he assumes that both the male and the female philosopher-rulers would learn not to be feminine in this way.

And yet at the same time there is the suggestion that feminine traits are acceptable if they cease to carry with them the implication that they are feminine. A clear example occurs in the *Phaedo*, when one of the officers who condemned Socrates to death weeps at the impending death of a man he has come to admire (116d). Earlier, Socrates had implored his friends to take his wife, Xanthippe, home because she "cried out and said the sort of thing that women usually say" (60b; see also 117d). But the officer's tears were not unwelcome and were not taken in any way to be a sign of effeminacy—perhaps not simply because they were being shed by a man, but also because he shed them in a becoming way, and they posed no threat of being unlimited, boundless, uncontrollable.

The significant correlation then is not between certain kinds of behavior and manliness or womanliness, but rather between the use of "feminine" to indicate disapproval of a form of behavior and "manly" to signal one's approval. Socrates and Thrasymachus disagree about what constitutes manly behavior—that is, right or appropriate behavior—but not about whether "manliness" is a term of praise. Similarly, Socrates' complaints about the poets to a degree are about what constitutes effeminate behavior, but he never doubts that the lovers of tragedy interpret "womanly" as a derogatory term; otherwise it would make no sense for him to try to convince them of the ill-effects of tragedy by associating grieving with what women do.

Given the central role women in classical Athens played in funeral rites as mourners, and vivid Socratic castigations of weeping and lamenting as womanish behavior, attempts in the *Republic* to mute grief appear to be aimed at minimizing powerful forms of typically feminine behavior. The virtual degriefing of the polis thus is a kind of de-feminizing of it. But this doesn't mean that Plato is suggesting that the price of containing grief is the elimination of women. Nor does it lead to the conclusion that he simply wanted them to be like men. An expression of grief is not necessarily womanly when expressed by a woman nor manly when expressed by a man. Although the description of behavior as manly never seems to have a negative valence, this does not mean that Plato was not involved in debates over what ought to count as manly behavior. Although the description of behavior as womanly never seems to have a positive valence, this does not mean that the behavior itself can't come to be seen as acceptable, even desirable. It means only that, should this happen, the behavior will not be describable as womanly. (As Martha Nussbaum has pointed out,[11] the Plato of the *Phaedrus* includes grief over the death of a loved one within the repertoire of acceptable emotions. Though no explicit attempt is made to rehabilitate the emotion as manly, there certainly is not a celebration of it as feminine.)

Just how free of grief does Plato expect the polis to be? Hope for an unambivalent picture is confounded by the tension in his depiction of the grounds of unity among polis members. When discussing what makes justice possible in the polis, and in individual members of it, Plato, as is well known, focuses on the division of labor among constituents of the state and of the soul. Rulers, auxiliaries, and artisans all have their specific functions in the state. When they acknowledge the necessity of that division and recognize their shared interests in not trying to do work other than that appropriate for their group, there will be no disharmony and disunity within the polis.[12] The same holds true for the three constituent parts of the soul: reason, spirit, appetite.

But, as we have also seen, at times the ground of unity in the polis is the shared grieving and rejoicing of everyone in the community, which implies a more positive and robust role for grief than that allowed for in the tripartite state and tripartite soul, where grief is portrayed as one of the capacities that threatens the control of the rational over the irrational.

Nevertheless, overall the *Republic* suggests that such grief should be contained and controlled. There are other, much more rational ways of organizing human life than those leading to the tragic events explored by the poets, or those that a Thrasymachus assumes would ensure individual human happiness. As long as there is grief, everyone should feel it on the same occasion for the same reason. But more generally, tempted as students of Homer and the tragedians may be to believe otherwise, suffering need not be the human condition. Such, at any rate, appears to be the lesson of the *Republic*.

The point of going over this lesson is not to try to decide whether Plato got grief right or whether his proposals for radically reducing the occasions of suffering are realistic or desirable. It is rather to see what he thought was at stake in getting grief right. It is an abrupt reminder that for Plato focusing on sufferers as subjects of tragedy amounts to a betrayal of them and a failure to live in accordance with our best selves. Such a focus, he insists, blinds us to the causes of human suffering, keeps us from doing anything useful about preventing further occasions of it, and indulges rather than checks or reduces our appetite-like capacity for grief. If nothing else, his claims are shockingly at odds with what appears to be a well-ingrained habit, at least in many Western cultures, of honoring the suffering of others by referring to it as tragic. In the next chapter we shall explore in more detail the question of how the rhetoric of tragedy shapes the economy of our attention to suffering.[13]

Chapter Two

SLAVERY AND TRAGEDY

*I*t takes but a peep into a daily newspaper, a turn of the television or radio dial, to note a favored device for trying to make us recognize significant suffering: "It's a tragedy," we are told, when a school bus slides down a mountainside, or when a whole town or city is devastated by an earthquake. Of course not all suffering is tragic, so not regarding someone's situation as tragic is not the same as disregarding it altogether or refusing to consider it as significant on other grounds, as in the suffering of martyrs, because of its presumed link to moral or religious ideals; or that of artists, on account of its alleged link to creativity. But in Western philosophical and literary traditions, describing suffering as tragic announces its claim on our attention. Suffering that deserves to be called tragic is noteworthy, in some sense exemplary, its threatening, chaotic horribleness diluted to some manageable degree by its riveting intelligibility.[1] There are grounds to hope that it will cease to be what Audre Lorde has called "unscrutinized and unmetabolized pain."[2]

Another historically powerful means of drawing attention to people's or groups' suffering is to describe them as slaves. For example, the comparison between the condition of slaves and the condition of women who were not slaves was a powerful trope in the campaigns for women's suffrage in the United States of the nineteenth century.[3] In what follows I consider the relationship between the kinds of suffering associated with tragedy (in some senses of that highly charged word) and that associated with slavery. Would it bring the proper kind of attention to the suffering of slaves to regard their plight as tragic? A close reading of Aristotle's views on both slavery and tragedy suggests that it might, since one indication of the subhuman status assigned slaves by Aristotle is their ineligibility for tragic heroic status. Apart from Aristotle, contemporary news reports make clear night after night that the significance afforded suffering is measured by the likelihood of its being thought of as tragic: the brutal rape and beating of a young white woman with a promising career on Wall Street is tragic, but similar events in the lives of Black or Hispanic women a few blocks away don't merit such an evaluation.

Against this background, it might seem a promising move indeed to refer to slavery in the United States as a tragedy for this country, perhaps as *the* American tragedy. Paradoxically, this turns out not to be the case; at least on one plausible understanding of such a claim, it does more to obscure than to reveal important dimensions of slavery. In coming to see why this is so, we can, I hope, learn more about some important senses of the tragic, and how they structure our understanding of slavery and other forms of suffering; we can see, as Aristotle himself would put it, what they teach us to be pained by, and why.

ARISTOTELIAN TRAGEDY

Aristotle's analysis of tragedy as a species of poetry has been much discussed and, according to most commentators, been badly misunderstood by almost everyone.[4] But we need not commit ourselves to hotly contested interpretations of central concepts and passages in order to see why an Aristotelian slave could not be the subject of an Aristotelian tragedy.

A tragedy, Aristotle tell us in the *Poetics*, is "the imitation [*mimēsis*] of an action that is serious and also, as having magnitude, complete in itself; in language with pleasurable accessories, each kind brought in separately in the parts of the work; in a dramatic, not in a narrative form; with incidents arousing pity and fear, wherewith to accomplish its catharsis of such emotions."[5]

The pity and fear requisite for the tragic effect will only occur—or should only occur[6]—if the action involves a particular kind of person who suffers misfortune for particular reasons. Tragedy must involve a man "not preeminently virtuous and just, whose misfortune, however, is brought upon him not by vice and depravity but by some fault [*hamartia*], a man of great reputation and prosperity, e.g. Oedipus, Thyestes, and the men of note of similar families. . . . [T]he change in the subject's fortunes must be . . . from good to bad; and the cause of it must lie not in any depravity, but in some great fault on his part; the man himself being either such as we have described, or better, not worse, than that."[7] Tragedy must depict "personages better than the ordinary man."[8]

(I shall use "man," "he," "him," and so on, in explicating Aristotle's views. On the one hand, though his task is not so much describing the structure of actual Greek tragedies as it is laying out normative criteria for good ones, he could hardly rule out the possibility of nonslave females as chief protagonists; but on the other hand, there is an uneasy fit between his profile of the tragic protagonist and that of his even "good" nonslave women.)

The tragic subject,[9] then, is a notably but not preeminently good person who suffers severe misfortune due to a fault, though not to a severe moral blemish, which contributes to but in no way shows he deserves the change in his fortunes. Were he simply a pitiable person, we wouldn't be surprised by what happens to him: it is just what we would expect to happen to such a perennial wretch. Were he less than a good man, we might have grounds for thinking he brought it on and thus deserves what happens to him; were he a man of extraordinary goodness, it would be difficult for us to imagine ourselves in his shoes, which is requisite for the fear and pity that, according to Aristotle, is crucial to tragedy. He must be enough like us for us to identify with him in some sense, but enough better than us to guarantee that his suffering is not deserved.

As John Kekes has reminded us, there is a difference between tragedy as a literary and dramatic genre and actual tragic situations.[10] Although Aristotle wrote about the former, not the latter, he nevertheless understood tragic poetry to illuminate the conditions of human life. He thought it does so not by referring to actual human lives, as history does, but by telling us about the kinds of events likely to be brought about by certain kinds of people in certain kinds of circumstances: "the poet's function is to describe, not the thing that has happened, but a kind of thing that might happen, i.e. what is possible as being probable or necessary."[11] Tragic poetry is about people who are recognizably human, but not in the way history is: "Poetry is something more philosophic and of graver import than history, since its statements are of the nature rather of universals, whereas those of history are singulars. By a universal I mean one as to what such or such a kind of man will probably or necessarily say or do."[12] The actions depicted must be in some sense recognizably human actions, even if not those actually performed by real historical agents, in order for them to arouse the necessary pity and fear.

If Aristotle believed tragedy tells us something significant, "of grave import," presumably he thought that we[13] can learn something from it about human life more generally, not just about a series of events in a single and unrepresentative life. Though Aristotle had a deep interest in human biology and anatomy, there is no reason to conclude that he meant *catharsis*, in the context of the *Poetics*, to involve only a kind of purgation in the medical sense. Readers of his *Nicomachean Ethics* know that for Aristotle a crucial aspect of developing the moral virtues is learning to have the right feelings in the right way at the right time toward the right people or events, for example (as we noted earlier), "to delight in and to be pained by the things that we ought."[14] Aristotle thinks that we should not have high regard for those who are ruled by their emotions, but he also says that we should praise "the man who is angry at the right things and with the right people, and, further, as he ought, when he ought, and as long as he ought."[15]

Good tragedy presumably will not simply arouse pity and fear but will do so in the right way, and we may thereby learn something about who and what it is appropriate for us to pity and fear. (It was because he was convinced that theatergoers could not learn to limit their grief and terror that Plato insisted on banning most forms of poetry from his ideal state.[16]) As Martha Nussbaum has put it, "Through attending to our responses of pity, we can hope to learn more about our own implicit view of what matters in human life, about the vulnerability of our own deepest commitments."[17] Hence, Nussbaum persuasively argues, the "catharsis" of emotion to which Aristotle refers is best understood not simply as a healthy release of pent-up feeling—Aristotle does not hold what Robert Solomon has described as the "hydraulic" model of emotion[18]—but rather as "a clarification (or illumination) concerning experiences of the pitiable and fearful kind."[19] One leaves a good tragedy not so much having spent one's emotions as having enlarged one's understanding of them and their appropriate place in human life.

An Aristotelian tragedy, then, is about exemplary human suffering. Not all suffering is exemplary, not all of it is representative of important facts about human life. By Aristotelian criteria (and here of course he is not alone), suffering is not tragic in and of itself. It cannot be trivial: it cannot be that of an insignificant or base person, nor even the minor trials and tribulations of a good if not "preeminently good" man. What makes a poetic account of such suffering universal is that it is about important kinds of things likely to happen to a certain kind of man; but such an account is not tragic unless it arouses the pity and fear of those who hear it.

It is important to note that what Aristotle means by "universal" here is *not* "it's the kind of thing that could and does happen to anyone." Aristotle doesn't say that what makes tragic poetry universal is that it is about what is likely to happen to *anyone*; what makes it universal is that it is about what is likely to happen to a particular kind of man—what universally or almost always happens to such a man. As is clear from the *Nicomachean Ethics* and the *Politics*, Aristotle was not in the habit of speaking about humans in general; there were for him crucial differences in kind among free men, free women, and slaves (male and female).[20] We would seriously misread his comments about universality in poetry if we thought he was saying that poetry, in comparison to history, is about everyone. This would be to ignore both what he says explicitly in the *Poetics* and his well-known views in the *Nicomachean Ethics* and the *Politics* about the differences among kinds of human beings.

What makes tragic events universal is not the same as what makes them exemplary. There are any number of universal statements that have no great import for human beings, particularly no tragic import. For example, Aristotle's works are full of universal statements about things such as baldness, sponges, and cuttlefish.[21] Whether a universal account of undeserved misfortune is also exemplary for human beings depends on whether the kind of man to whom such undeserved misfortune falls is also the kind of person that members of the audience take themselves to be; in the absence of such an identification, the necessary pity and fear will be lacking.

ARISTOTELIAN SLAVES
AS NONTRAGIC FIGURES

Now we are in a position to see why we need not settle centuries-old debates about the meaning of *mimēsis*, *hamartia*, or *catharsis* in the *Poetics* in order to see why an Aristotelian slave could not be the subject of an Aristotelian tragedy (which is not to say that Aristotle imagined no role at all for slaves in tragedy).[22]

As we have seen, Aristotle describes the protagonist of a good tragedy as "not preeminently virtuous and just" yet "better than the ordinary man."[23] This means that the tragic protagonist cannot be so much better than we are that we can feel neither pity nor fear for him. On the other hand, a thoroughly base and wicked person, however universal the events that follow on his actions, couldn't be a tragic protagonist either: pity, Aristotle says, "is occasioned by undeserved misfortune, and fear by that of one like ourselves."[24] We aren't likely to pity (and in any event shouldn't pity) wicked people since we aren't likely to believe their misfortune is undeserved; we aren't likely to fear that what happens to the wicked will happen to us unless—a possibility Aristotle implicitly excludes—we take ourselves to be among the wicked.

But a whole class of individuals exists who couldn't possibly be tragic protagonists: those whom Aristotle refers to as "slaves by nature." These are different from the men and women whom Aristotle describes as "slaves by convention"[25]—the convention according to which conquered people are among the booty taken by their victors. Slaves by nature are men and women who ought to be ruled by others; tossed only a tiny dose of rationality by nature, they are able to understand the orders of their natural rulers but are incapable of deliberation about their own or others' lives; very much like animals, their natural function is "to minister to the needs of life."[26]

What makes such slaves ineligible for tragic status is not their being among the "preeminently good and just," those whose excellence so exceeds ours that we couldn't possibly connect their possible misfortunes with our own. Nor do they lack potential tragic status because they are among the wicked and base whose misfortunes we would have difficulty regarding as undeserved. Slaves are capable of their own kind of goodness, Aristotle tells us: "goodness is possible in every kind of personage, even in a woman or a slave" (that is, even in a free woman or a male or female slave).[27] But a woman, that is, a nonslave female, Aristotle immediately adds, is "perhaps an inferior," and a slave "a wholly worthless being."[28] (Even if in this context Aristotle is referring to conventional slaves, we can be sure the comment applies with even more force to natural slaves.) Such slaves are not without value, Aristotle tells us in the *Politics*: their work is necessary for the polis to exist. But they have nothing to contribute to the essential deliberative activities engaged in by even the most ordinary male citizens.[29] We have nothing to learn from charting their misfortunes; their faults could not possibly be interesting or instructive.

While the tragic protagonist is not a paragon of intellectual or moral virtue,[30] he nonetheless is capable of considerable deliberation; indeed a temporary failure or blindness in deliberation could constitute a tragic fault (Oedipus, we recall, went out of his way to try to avoid killing his father and sleeping with his mother). But a slave doesn't have enough rational capacity for his faults along these or other lines to be emblematic. At most, Aristotle implies, the faults in a slave in which we might be interested are cowardice and lack of self-control, but only because they can undermine the particular kind of excellence necessary for the slave to perform his function in the polis.[31] As a minimally ratiocinated beast of burden, a slave is not someone to whom we can attach eventful actions of the sort which tragedy is to depict.

From Aristotle's perspective it doesn't even make sense to speak of the slave as suffering misfortune simply on account of being a slave. Aristotle's criteria for the tragic protagonist, in the strict sense of the *Poetics*, preclude the idea that being born a slave, being a slave by nature, is tragic. For even if one were to regard being a slave by nature a misfortune, it is not the kind of misfortune that we can trace to a tragic fault.[32] And Aristotle didn't seem to think that on any grounds being a natural slave is a misfortune. Perhaps he thanked his lucky stars he was not a slave,[33] but he certainly didn't think the fact of natural slavery was regrettable. As we have seen, Aristotle thought slaves were necessary for the life of the polis, and that there were ways for slaves, as for all other groups, to perform their functions well and in that sense lead a good life. He wished others to see that slavery is natural and necessary and hence not a misfortune, and surely not a tragic situation that rightly arouses

43

our pity and fear and produces a catharsis, or a clarification of them.

Indeed, on Aristotelian grounds there is no reason to think slaves would be the appropriate object of either our pity or our fear, or of the particular pity and fear good tragedy evokes. We—even if "we" are slaves—can't, or anyway shouldn't, pity them for having to spend their lives doing hard labor under the direction of others, since the labor is necessary, should not be done by citizens,[34] and is what slaves were intended by nature to do. This is not to say that slaves cannot be mistreated, only that being obliged to perform strenuous labor at the command of others is not mistreatment if that is precisely what you are most fit for.

And if we only can, or only should, pity those who are "one of us," then Aristotle would hardly think slaves would, or should, be the object of pity of citizens, since he emphasizes the difference in kind between citizens and slaves. "The difference between ruler and subject is a difference of kind, which the difference of more and less never is."[35] Citizens who are themselves capable of ruling could hardly fear that what happens to slaves could happen to them; or if they did, the fear would be highly unreasonable, because however slovenly or intemperate or irrational a member of the class of natural rulers grows, he can't change the natural difference between himself and a slave. Perhaps he could fear coming to be treated like a slave, but it would make no sense for him to fear becoming a slave. However great his faults, he cannot initiate actions that result in his becoming a natural slave.

John Gassner overstated the case when he argued that "[Aristotelian] tragedy involves our capacity to feel for others and fear for ourselves, too, by knowing that we share in their humanity and that they share in ours, which rules out the possibility of our ever dismissing humane considerations concerning other members of the species."[36] If we don't regard this as an overstatement, then we must assume either that he forgot that Aristotle made rigid distinctions among humans, or that he shared Aristotle's view that it is not inhumane to regard some members of the species as slaves by nature and to treat them accordingly.

In sum, according to Aristotle, if we are citizens we needn't pity slaves simply for being slaves nor fear developing into natural slaves ourselves; and because their faults, and the events of their lives, neither of which could ever arise above the trivial, are so different from ours, we could never be moved to pity and fear in contemplating them. Neither the state of slavery nor the events in slaves' lives could be grist for the mill of tragedy. Again, it is important to remember that tragic poetry is universal according to Aristotle not in the sense that it concerns events likely to unfold in the life of just anyone but in the sense that it is about events likely to unfold in the life of a certain kind of man (or perhaps a certain kind of woman). Though such a man may be neither of surpassing goodness nor of base vileness, he cannot be a natural slave. Slaves lack potential tragic standing, even though presumably they could be among those caught in the wake of events precipitated by the actions of a tragically flawed central personage. (A tragedy involves lots of people, but that doesn't mean they all play a crucial role in causing it.)

It is true that Aristotle does not explicitly exclude slaves from his list of possible tragic protagonists, but it wouldn't occur to him that he needed to do so. As he conceived them, slaves were only of instrumental value to the polis, hardly the stuff for a "presentation of human destiny"[37] or for an exploration of "the many ways in which being of a certain good human character falls short of sufficiency for *eudaimonia*."[38] For "the narrow and trivial life of obscure persons cannot give scope for a great and significant action, one of tragic consequence."[39]

Aristotelian tragedy makes human faults interesting and renders human suffering somehow redeemable by giving it a particular kind of intelligibility. Aristotle's exclusion of what he calls "natural slaves" reveals the depth of the "social death" of such slaves (the concept is borrowed from Orlando Patterson, though I use it somewhat differently here).[40] We know from the *Politics* that slaves are not to be considered part of the community of citizens; it is also clear in this work that the distinction between male and female that matters so much to Aristotle when discussing forms of polities concerns him not at all when discussing slaves.[41] Juxtaposing these and related passages to the treatment of tragedy in the *Poetics*, we see a further mark of slaves' exclusion from the versions of humanity that are said to matter most. The suffering of slaves cannot be properly taken up by tragedy. But it is not simply because they are slaves that we needn't attend to their pain, for it is not as if they suffer like other people but we're just not supposed to pay attention to it. The very meaning of their suffering, indeed the very possibility of it at all, is shaped by the fact of their being slaves. Slaves don't have enough rationality for them to be either really good or really evil; instead of tragic faults they have permanent limitations. They aren't beings for whom the notions of tragically deserved or undeserved suffering can take hold in any significant way. What they do suffer they undergo dumbly, like the brute animals they otherwise resemble in function.

SLAVERY AS "THE AMERICAN TRAGEDY"

Whatever his shortcomings as a thoroughgoing critic of racism,[42] Mark Twain saw clearly that part of being a slave—whether or not this was given Aristotelian grounding[43]—is that even one's pain doesn't deserve notice, that the important stories of human suffering don't include one's own. In *Huckleberry Finn*, Mrs. Phelps is relieved to hear that no one really got hurt in a reported explosion; all that happened was that a Black man was killed.[44] Twain, of course, means to indict even "good whites" for the failure to notice or be moved by the suffering of their Black neighbors. The fictional Mrs. Phelps's casual dismissal of the pain and sorrow of Blacks was given fuller articulation and justification by a host of nonfictional whites, such as Dr. Samuel A. Cartwright, a physician on Louisiana plantations in the 1840s who proclaimed that Blacks just don't have the sensitivity to pain and suffering that whites have; by the novelist Mrs. Henry Schoolcraft, who encouraged whites to believe that it wasn't possible to work a slave too hard; by the Georgian Thomas R. R. Cobb, who meant to spare whites any misgivings they might have about breaking up slave families by insisting that slaves weren't capable of the kind of familial affection that could make such separation painful.[45]

Such lack of desire to note and try to understand what slavery meant to slaves was echoed until recently in most professional historical accounts of the period. Reviewing U. B. Phillips's *American Negro Slavery* in 1919, critic Carter G. Woodson remarked on Phillips's willingness to overplay the benevolence of slave owners and "his inability to fathom the negro mind"; indeed, according to Woodson, "In just the same way as a writer of the history of New England in describing the fisheries of that section would have little to say about the species figuring conspicuously in that industry, so has the author treated the negro in his work."[46] Only decades later did the historical profession begin to try to depict slavery from the perspectives of the slaves themselves.[47]

Against this pervasive and long-enduring background of callous indifference to the many dimensions of slaves' lives, including the meaning of their suffering, it seems tempting to applaud the historian George M. Frederickson's reference to "the tragic limitation of the white racial imagination of the nineteenth century, namely its characteristic inability to visualize an egalitarian biracial society."[48] The juxtaposition of the idea of tragedy with the history of slavery and racism in the United States seems to encourage us to take the suffering of slaves seriously, seems to reflect the belief that such suffering commands attention both for its own sake and because of its significance for the meaning of the founding vision of American society and influential white American thought in the nineteenth century. The call for liberty and equality in the name of which was declared independence from the British Crown was, of course, severely limited: it did not include the male and female slaves by whose labor, according to at least one prominent historian, Americans "bought their independence."[49] Most white Americans did not, many perhaps still do not, worry about the inconsistency nor notice the suffering at the center of a society reputed to be founded on freedom and independence.[50] So it would seem to be no small change in view for Frederickson not only to point to the "limitation" built into the powerful notion of equality but to describe it as tragic. But where does the rhetorical device of talking about "the tragic limitation" of that vision actually take us? Does it really point us to the experience of slaves at all, and if so, how?

I do not wish to saddle George Frederickson with a view unwarranted by comments that he made in the preface to one of his many fine books on the history of race and race relations in the United States. So I shall describe the view I wish to examine not as something attributable to Frederickson but as something suggested by his words.

White racism, but particularly its expression in slavery, is an American (that is, U.S.) tragedy, perhaps *the* American tragedy.[51] It is only through the kind of failing that, following Aristotle roughly, we might call tragic, that those grand enough to endorse freedom and equality could not see the ways in which the slavery they condoned undermined the promise of freedom, or foresee that at the very moment they planted the seeds of a new nation, they also laid the groundwork for its failure to fully realize equality. The assumption that only through some enormous mistake or unexpected failure could slavery be found in this new safe harbor of freedom is so powerful that one influential student of slavery felt it was necessary to begin his book on the topic by pointing out that "there is nothing in the least anomalous about the fact that [someone as strongly committed to freedom as] a Jefferson owned slaves."[52]

Thinking of slavery as the American tragedy suggests, in a semi-Aristotelian way, that there is a flaw in the founding vision of America but that it is otherwise noble and powerful. An impoverished or mean vision of human society, a vision with obvious shortcomings, could hardly have its failings described as "tragic"; the disastrous consequences likely to flow from it would be all too obvious, all too deserved. To use "tragic" in this context calls our attention to the grandness of the vision even while, indeed by means of, noting a not-so-obvious fault corked into it. "Tragic" also suggests the hideously compelling strength of the forces that revealed or produced its failures; forces like these must be interesting if they can wreak that kind of havoc. It is not a faulty vision, but a splendid vision with a hidden fault.

But from what perspective, from whose perspective, is the "inability to visualize a biracial egalitarian society" *tragic*? It cannot be tragic from the viewpoint of those white Americans, then and now, who did or do not believe in the equality of Blacks and whites. While such Americans may well believe that injustices have been born by Blacks, they do not think that white supremacy per se involves unjust suffering that can be traced to unfortunate faults in whites. Indeed, from the perspective of some white Americans, the real tragic limitation of nineteenth-century America was the inability of the devotees of racial egalitarianism to foresee the dire effects of Reconstruction. Now *that*, the historian Claude G. Bowers wrote in an influential book by the same title, brought about "the tragic era," sounding the "death-knell of civilization in the South."[53]

But from another perspective, describing white America's "inability to visualize an egalitarian society" as a "tragic limitation" points to the enormous consequences in terms of suffering that limitation entailed. However, insofar as "tragic limitation" suggests that white America had good intentions that failed to be realized through all-too-human faults, there is good reason to balk at such a characterization, in fact, to be deeply suspicious of it.

As a rhetorical device, the concept of the tragic frames the relation between freedom and slavery in U.S. history in a distinctive way. This becomes clear when we note what it obscures, and if we consider other means of depicting that relation.

1. The idea of slavery as the American tragedy simply elides the well-known fact that those who forged the notion of a society peopled by free citizens standing on equal footing with one another never intended to include slaves (among others) among those citizens. If some whites thought otherwise, Blacks had far fewer incentives to be deceived.

2. To frame the relation between the freedom envisioned by the Founding Fathers and the slavery with which that freedom coexisted in terms of tragedy simply recasts slaves in the subordinate relation to their masters that slavery enforced. In much the same ways in which some white Americans' enjoyment of life, liberty, and the pursuit of happiness was predicated on the slavery of Black Americans, the tragic stature of the founding ideals is predicated on the suffering inherent in slavery. While referring to the limited vision of influential whites as "tragic" does invite us to think about the suffering it entailed, the vision's being tragic salvages it. After all, one can't be a tragic character unless one has the interesting and powerful kind of faults

51

that can wreak havoc on others. Tragedies do not simply require the pain of innocent victims produced by the flaws of an otherwise good person; they suggest that this is a cost that can perhaps be redeemed by the insight it gives us about the human condition.

Whose suffering is redeemed by calling it tragic? Surely not that of the nameless numbers of people affected by the outcome of the behavior of the troubled central character. It is not their condition for which we feel pity and fear, but that of the interesting wretch who put all this in motion. The instructive suffering of tragedy—at least on a more or less Aristotelian view—is that of the person who realizes how he or she has brought about disaster, not those who through no fault, and hence no interesting fault, happen to be affected by our dear hero or heroine.

A parallel with Aristotle will be helpful here. Aristotle doesn't say this explicitly, but surely a failure on the part of the person in whom the flaw occurs to become aware of that flaw and thus of his role in bringing about the disastrous consequences would cancel one crucial element of tragedy. The tragic hero doesn't know, can't know[54] at the particular time that the apparently harmless, innocent, or even intentionally helpful action he has taken will, given the rest of the relevant circumstances, spell disaster for many concerned. But if they never discover it, and go on their merry way without recognizing the significance of their actions, or if they discover it, and yet aren't deeply disturbed by it, surely there is no tragedy in the Aristotelian sense, no matter how horrible the consequences. However much we may pity the victims of the hero's acts, we cannot pity the hero if he is not deeply pained by the recognition of his role in bringing about such consequences. If he lacks the capacity to recognize his role or to suffer from such recognition, or, having such capacity, fails in this case to understand his part and be mortified by it, he cannot have the goodness requisite for a tragic personage.

If slavery is the American tragedy, then even though attention is directed to the suffering of slaves, the real subjects of tragedy nonetheless are some white Americans, good and grand enough of heart and mind to envision an egalitarian society, but also and necessarily good and grand enough ultimately to recognize and be pained by their own flaws and the wretched effect of them on Black Americans. How tragic, to be so great and yet so deeply implicated in the pain of others.

There is quite a difference between "Nobody knows the trouble I've seen" and "Everyone knows the trouble I've made."

3. Although describing American slavery as tragic in light of the founding vision of equality and freedom is insisting on the appropriateness of being pained by the remissness of American society to live up to such a vision, it is also to frame that failure as something for which powerful white Americans, beginning with the Founding Fathers, are to be excused even as they are held responsible. It is their flaws, for sure, that contributed so much to ensuing suffering, but insofar as it makes sense to refer to those flaws as tragic, the disapprobation that might otherwise be forthcoming is not quite fitting, for at least two reasons. First, for the most part, tragic figures—those who cause suffering rather than those who simply are the victims—regret and are deeply pained by what they have done.[55] Second, typically they are their own harshest critics, so to call American slavery tragic is to take judgment out of the hands of those who

suffered, for such criticism has been preempted by those who realize what they have done. In this connection Oedipus' painful self-awareness and self-blame are illustrative. About the extent of his responsibility, Oedipus offers the judgment: "[Apollo] brought my sick, sick fate upon me / But the blinding hand was my own; . . . This punishment / That I have laid upon myself is just." About the weight of such a burden, Oedipus expresses the belief that "of all men, I alone can bear this guilt."[56]

4. The ways in which characterizing slavery as the American tragedy puts a good face on an ugly fact becomes particularly clear when we think about alternative descriptions of the existence of slavery in "a country which saw itself—and was perceived by others—as the standard-bearer of liberty and democracy."[57] Peter Parish, in his recent book on the historiography of slavery, refers to the existence of slavery in the American republic alternatively as "a malignant tumor," an "irony," and a "paradox."[58] While neither "irony" nor "paradox" points us in the direction of those who suffered under slavery, each nonetheless does less to glorify the failures of a white supremacist America than does tragedy, for each suggests that the failure of vision at issue is something to be embarrassed by, not something that can be parlayed into a compellingly interesting fault. "Malignant tumor" cancels human agency and responsibility, but at the same time raises doubts about the idea of noble or good origins so strongly suggested by "tragic."

The concept of the tragic encourages us to think of freedom-loving slaveholding whites as noble though flawed figures, struggling gallantly to live by their principles but unable finally to do what they believe is right. This makes it difficult to imagine other descriptions of their struggles with conflicting values, such as the following.

While some slave owners no doubt were dogged by a sense of sinfulness, there was much to mitigate the pain of such awareness: "If we do commit a *sin* owning slaves, it is certainly one which is attended with great *conveniences*."[59]

Not all tension is painful: "As humans, masters were by definition complex beings, capable of holding to contradictory values, motivated by principles at odds with their behavior, torn by irreconcilable impulses intrinsic to their way of life. . . . Among its many rewards, slavery offered masters the luxury of ambivalence."[60]

From the perspective of many slaves, the institution of slavery was not so much a matter of ambivalence as a readiness to live by double standards. Note Frederick Douglass: "But it has been said that negroes are not included within the benefits sought under [the Constitution]. This is said by the slaveholders in America—it is said by the City Hall orator—but it is not said by the Constitution itself. Its language is 'we the people'; not the white people, not even we the citizens, not we the privileged class, not we the high, not we the low, but we the people."[61]

According to James Baldwin, writing a century after Douglass, such betrayal and mockery of the official creed of the Republic was not confined to the eighteenth or nineteenth century: "The Negro's experience of the white world cannot possibly create in him any respect for the standards by which the white world claims to live. His own condition is overwhelming proof that white people do not live by those standards."[62]

Baldwin both pities and fears many white Americans, but

not because he is moved by the perception of a tragic flaw. He pities "spineless" whites, he says, "in order not to despise them."[63]

5. Among the most troubling of the implications of viewing slavery as the American tragedy—and this is part of the close attention to whites it entails—is that it focuses on the short-comings of whites rather than the strengths of Blacks. Indeed it makes the shortcomings of whites much more interesting than the strength of Blacks. The suffering that tragedy brings to our attention in this context includes that of slaves, but only as vic-tims; whites are only "victims" of their own faults, which are the intriguingly distressing center of the tragedy, faults the possession of which distinguishes the agents of the tragedy from its innocent victims. To refer to the victims of suffering as tragic can only be to register one's sense of the magnitude of their suffering; it does not invite inquiry into the details of their lives, in particular, into their responses to being in that sit-uation.[64]

Under what conditions, then, is one's suffering redeemed or at least mitigated by its presentation as part of a tragic situa-tion? Against the background of the idea that slavery really was good for slaves, and that what they endured wasn't torturous because they were not nearly as sensitive to physical and emo-tional pain as whites, some of the horrors of slavery are perhaps leached out if one includes slaves as part of a tragic situation. But that still makes slaves bit players in the drama of American history. And insofar as the notion of the tragic suggests inevita-ble human powerlessness in the face of overwhelming forces, it makes the spiritual resources of slaves seem pointless. It deprives W. E. B. Du Bois of the point of praising slaves for sustaining a quite untragic hope of freedom "for two centuries," in the face of a system of slavery that was the "sum of all villainies, the cause of all sorrow, the root of all prejudice."[65] The fact that white people and white institutions were the cause of Black suffering under slavery did not mean that when Blacks envisioned the end of such suffering, they included whites in their images of the future. Although the notion of slavery as the American tragedy acknowledges the role of whites in the suffering of Blacks, it does not allow for Blacks to make sense of and go through and beyond that suffering independently of whites. Slavery as tragedy brought on by whites leaves no room for the possibility that furthest from the minds and hearts of many slaves in terms of a redemptive vision was the image of tragically flawed whites owning up to their faults: "In the world of the spirituals, it was not the masters and mistresses but God and Jesus and the entire pantheon of Old Testament figures who set the standards, established the precedents, and defined the values; who, in short, constituted the 'significant others.' The world described by the slave songs was a black world in which no reference was ever made to any white contemporaries."[66]

To say this is not to forget that spiritual resources called upon by slaves to try to come to terms with their oppression were quite capable of deepening it, through what Du Bois, for example, called the "doctrines of passive submission embodied in the newly learned Christianity."[67] But to acknowledge the situation of slaves by linking it to the tragic limitations of whites ensures that Blacks are not talked about independently of whites. The suffering of slaves remains the property of the tragically flawed characters and institutions that caused it.

Is thinking of slavery in terms of an American tragedy a plausible and promising way of bringing attention to the experiences of slaves? The rhetoric of tragedy, at least in an Aristotelian mode, in this context turns out to lead mainly in quite other directions. While acknowledging the suffering of Blacks, it hovers around whites, not despite but because of their limitations; it redeems and articulates the anguish involved in doing wrong rather than that of having wrong done to one; it holds whites responsible for the suffering of Blacks in such a way as also ultimately to excuse them; it preempts the most biting criticism of whites by Blacks; and it obscures the spiritual resources of Blacks for dealing with suffering independently of their relationship to whites.

Tragedy is powerful stuff. Before applauding its appearance, we might ask, paradoxically echoing Aristotle: over whom, over what, do we grieve, and why?[68]

THE HEADY POLITICAL LIFE
OF COMPASSION

*O*ne important function of slave
narratives and other critical depictions of North American slavery was to generate compassion in their audiences, provoke the kind of feeling that would incline readers to help relieve suffering and oppose evil. In *Incidents in the Life of a Slave Girl, Written by Herself*, the ex-slave Harriet Jacobs, writing under the pseudonym Linda Brent, expresses hope that she can "kindle a flame of compassion in your hearts for my sisters who are still in bondage, suffering as I once suffered." Having been so moved, perhaps readers will cease being silent and join others "laboring to advance the cause of humanity."[1]

But as Harriet Jacobs herself well understood, far from tending to undermine the master-slave relation, kindly feelings of various sorts may simply reflect and reinforce it. For example, the white abolitionist Angelina Grimké exposed the political logic of certain emotions when she rightly read the "pity" and "generosity" of certain whites as indicative of their "regard[ing] the colored man as an *unfortunate inferior*, rather than as an *outraged and insulted equal*."[2] Frances Ellen Watkins Harper found it necessary to insist, in an 1891 speech to the National Council of Women of the United States, that she came "to present the negro, not as a mere dependent asking for Northern sympathy or Southern compassion, but as a member of the body politic who has a claim upon the nation for justice, simple justice."[3]

So while Harriet Jacobs was in part hoping to arouse compassion and concern in an apathetic and neglectful white audience, like Grimké and Harper she was aware that appeals for compassion could be politically problematic. *Incidents* is a political text not simply because it is meant to get its audience to challenge existing institutions but also because it constitutes an ex-slave's struggle against readings of her experiences of slavery that would reflect and reinforce the master-slave relationship. Indeed, we cannot adequately understand the plea for compassion in *Incidents in the Life of a Slave Girl* unless we look at Jacobs's ongoing attempts throughout the text to assert and maintain authority over the meaning of her suffering. As Mary Helen Washington has pointed out, narratives such as Jacobs's exhibit slave women as "active agents rather than objects of pity."[4] Jacobs wants her audience's compassion, but she wants that compassion to be well informed. She needs to have the members of her audience understand that she and others are suffering, but she is highly attuned to the power that their knowledge of her suffering can give them, and so she simultaneously instructs them how to feel. She insists on her right to have an authoritative—though not unchallengeable—take on the meaning of her suffering.

Jacobs is aware of the debates going on over her suffering. She knows that something is at stake in the determination of the nature of her pain, its causes, its consequences, its relative weight, its moral, religious, and social significance. And if there is such an explicit or implicit struggle, the meaning of her pain is not a given. Competing interpretations are possible, and something important hangs on which interpretation or interpretations prevail.

For the meaning of someone's pain to be debatable in these ways is to give it a place in what Hannah Arendt referred to as the "public realm," that is, for the pain to be a topic about which different people may well have different views, and thus for it to be among the items constituting a common, public world for these people not despite the fact but precisely because of the fact that their separateness is thereby revealed. Like Harriet Jacobs, though in another context a century later, Hannah Arendt was deeply interested in the relationship between compassion and political action. But in Arendt's account the kind of debate over the meaning of suffering which I have described as a crucial context of *Incidents* cannot even take place, for the kind of pain to which compassion is an appropriate response is not something over which varying perspectives are even possible. Moreover, according to Arendt public professions of concern about the suffering of others are by their very nature bound to degenerate into pity, which accentuates the distance and inequality between those in pain and those exhibiting feeling for them. By Arendt's lights, Harriet Jacobs's invocation of the compassion of northern white women runs the serious risk of simply reinforcing the very forms of inequality Jacobs hoped her plea would begin to undermine. Let us see why. Then we will be in a position to appreciate what Jacobs did in order to minimize that risk.

HANNAH ARENDT

In *The Human Condition* Hannah Arendt describes intense physical pain as the "most private" and "least communicable" of human experiences.[5] The degree to which something is "private" in the relevant sense, Arendt says, is the degree to which it can appear in public, the degree to which it can be seen or heard or otherwise come to the notice of and become a topic of conversation for others and oneself. Physical pain by its very nature, Arendt seems to be saying, is such that only with great difficulty can it be "transformed ... for public appearance." Thus, however intense it may be, in an important sense it lacks reality—the kind of reality only talking about experience can provide (*HC*, 45–47).

On the other hand, in *On Revolution* Arendt certainly doesn't doubt that we can know that others are in pain, miserable, in constant want, or in a state of humiliation.[6] Indeed she reminds us that the "spectacle" of others' misery can be right before us and yet we can fail to see it or be moved by it (*OR*, 70). This appears to contradict her claims in *The Human Condition*, but there is a coherent position that emerges from a close reading of these and related texts.

First of all, in *The Human Condition* Arendt is focusing particularly on intense physical pain, and while such pain is often an ingredient of misery, want, and humiliation, the latter states are not identical to physical pain. Arendt doesn't say that it is impossible, but only difficult, to communicate what she describes as the most private kind of pain. What concerns her is not an epistemological worry that we cannot know or speak about the pain and suffering of others (or of ourselves), but rather a moral and political worry about what happens to the experience of suffering and the responses to it when it becomes publicly discussed. Arendt is most emphatic about keeping private experiences private—a concern that would make no sense at all if she thought they could only remain private anyway.

Arendt, then, has no doubt that we are capable not only of being made aware of the suffering of others but of being moved by what we know or believe about their experience.[7] But she insists that our concern for their suffering cannot become public, cannot become discussed, surely cannot become professed, without becoming dangerously distorted. For her the prime example of such inevitable mangling of feeling is Robespierre's celebration of compassion for *le peuple* (*OR*, 75 ff.) To feel real compassion for another, Arendt says—and she has no doubt that there are examples of real compassion—is to be "stricken" with the suffering of a particular person (*OR*, 85). One is so much a cosufferer that the ordinary distance between oneself and the sufferer is abolished. Since it is precisely this distance that both allows for and requires joint talk—the joint talk which creates the common world between us—compassion is marked by a kind of mutedness (*OR*, 86). In this state of mutedness, one has neither the inclination nor the capacity to engage in the kind of deliberation and discussion that, according to

Arendt, constitutes our public and political lives together. Hence, Arendt says, while compassion is not generally characterized by readiness to speak or act,[8] people in the throes of compassion who do act "will shun the long drawn-out processes of persuasion and will lend their voice to suffering, which has to claim swift action and violence" (*OR*, 86).

Thus, according to Arendt, whatever feeling Robespierre may have had for those in the name of whose suffering he spoke and acted quickly degenerated into something ugly, false, and dangerous when he and others began to profess it. Robespierre's description of the object of such feeling as *le peuple* is very telling. It reveals that whatever he feels cannot be compassion, because by its nature compassion is something one feels for a particular person (*OR*, 85).[9] The use of *le peuple* also indicates that those who are the objects of the alleged feeling have had no say in the presentation of who they are and what they are going through: the connotations of *le peuple* were determined "by those exposed to the spectacle of sufferings they did not share" (*OR*, 75). That is, the profession of the feeling of compassion for "the people" reveals a kind of loquacity on the part of those professing such feeling, an attempt to put forth an authoritative interpretation of the experiences of those suffering, to enter into the public record not only that *le peuple* are suffering but what their suffering means, and to announce one's virtue by registering one's feeling about such suffering. By making one's feeling public, one offers proof of the depth of one's connection with those who are in such great pain and thus the right to speak about and for them. And since such pain is, under the circumstances, part and parcel of the virtue of *le peuple*, *les malheureux*, to present oneself as suffering with them while not one of

64

them became crucial evidence of one's possessing virtue as well (*OR*, 75, 111).

By Arendt's lights, such profession of compassion actually amounts to pity, which involves both a looser and a tighter connection to those who are suffering than does compassion: looser, in the sense that in pity for *le peuple* one feels sorry for a faceless or many-faced multitude; one is not "touched in the flesh" (*OR*, 85) by any particular sufferer. And insofar as pity, unlike compassion, is not a matter of cosuffering, it heightens rather than erases differences between the nonsuffering and the suffering. Yet pity also has a tighter connection to sufferers than compassion: insofar as pity can so easily come to be enjoyed for its own sake, the pitier needs and seeks out others in misfortune. The suffering of others is not borne by the pitier but kept dangling at a delicious and cruel distance (*OR*, 89).

Now we are in a position to see what I referred to earlier as Arendt's moral and political worry about the experience of suffering and the responses to it when they become public matters. She has several closely related concerns here. One is that professions of compassion all too often are barely disguised forms of pity, that what is presented as an authentic and spontaneous concern for another human being is actually a selfish and cruel wallowing in the misfortunes of others. While compassion's object is the suffering of another, pity uses the suffering of another—any old other will do—to produce or prolong a feeling in oneself.

Another reason Arendt is doubtful about linking compassion to political life is that, as she sees it, to feel compassion is to have a stance toward someone's suffering that is completely at odds with what political life requires. A compassionate response to someone's suffering, Arendt is implying, is a response that leaves no doubt about the fact of or the meaning of that suffering. If there are no doubts or uncertainties or optional responses, there is no reason to discuss, deliberate, make decisions. To make an issue of another's suffering or of one's response to it suggests that the fact of the other's suffering, the meaning of it, or the existence of one's own response to it, has yet to be determined, and that one is weighing in with one's own views about these matters. The reason we tend to doubt professions of care and compassion (see, for example, *HC* 47, *OR* 96 ff.), she implies, is that the possibility of the absence of such feeling is suggested by the mere presence of public words about it. For something to be in the public eye means it is part of the world we jointly inhabit and about which we therefore can and will have different perspectives. When experiencing compassion, one doesn't make whether someone is suffering a matter of public debate, or a matter about which there will be many possible interpretations. It is in this sense that for Arendt compassion is so thoroughly apolitical, antipolitical. She has high regard for real compassion, especially in comparison with its cruel sister, pity; but compassion is by definition not part of public, political life. The perception of suffering that informs real compassion is too sure, too impervious to alteration, to be open to the possible change of opinion, open to the challenge to its claim to truth, which for Arendt is constitutive of public and political life.[10]

Another reason for Arendt's separation of compassion and political activity is that in its definitive form, political life consists not merely of equals engaged in "discussions, deliberations, decisions" (*OR*, 119), but their doing so in order to "be seen, heard, talked of, approved and respected" by people they know and regard as their worthy competitors (*OR*, 119). Arendt celebrates this desire to excel, and she takes pains to distinguish such an aspiration from the snuffing out of competing parties and competing views that characterizes tyranny and other invidious forms of domination (*OR*, 119). But she implicitly assumes we would share her distaste, disdain, and distrust of anyone who wished to excel at compassion, who extolled and claimed to exemplify compassion as a political virtue (*OR*, 75).

So for Arendt there appear to be only two kinds of emotional responses to suffering, and neither has a place in public and political life. On the one hand, one might be so "stricken" with the suffering of another that one suffers as the other does, bears the suffering of the other. Such sharing precludes or obviates the need for deliberation and discussion that are definitive of public life. On the other hand, one can feel for the suffering of another in a way that reflects and announces the distance between nonsufferer and sufferer. But this doesn't open up public space, because the nonsufferer doesn't allow the sufferer a particular face or a particular voice. So if in the first case there is not the variety of perspectives characteristic of public life because two potential subjects have been collapsed into one by the fact of cosuffering, in the second case there is not a variety of perspectives because one subject makes himself or herself into a ventriloquist for the other. Arendt calls the first kind of situation "compassion" and the second one "pity."

The important point here is not whether Arendt has given us the correct definition of these terms; indeed, what she calls "compassion" many others would call "empathy,"[11] and in everyday English "compassion" and "pity" often are used interchangably. Nor is my aim to present Hannah Arendt as the final word on the proper domain of politics, the motives of Robespierre, or the political significance of the French Revolution.[12] But the questions she raises about the phenomena she identifies as compassion and pity vividly alert us to some of the risks Harriet Jacobs took in invoking the compassion of the white women who were her intended audience. For though Jacobs understood compassion in a somewhat different way than Arendt, she was aware that in encouraging northern white women to exercise their capacity for compassion, she might instead be creating occasions for them to feel good without doing anything about slavery; she was concerned that her own voice and that of other slaves might be drowned out in the battle between northern and southern whites over what the suffering of slaves meant.

However, as we now shall see, Jacobs does not share Arendt's view that the only way to avoid such risks is to keep emotional life separate from political life, nor Arendt's insistence that what we feel (or don't feel) for sufferers is something that should not become part of what we discuss and debate. Jacobs assumes, on the contrary, that debates over the meaning of the suffering of slaves were shaped by and were shaping what people felt or didn't feel, and she thought it crucial to be part of those debates.

LINDA BRENT

Harriet Jacobs published *Incidents in the Life of a Slave Girl, Written by Herself*, in 1861.[13] Jacobs had by this time been living in the North almost twenty years, having escaped from North Carolina in 1842. At the suggestion of the white abolitionist Amy Post, Jacobs, using the pseudonym Linda Brent, began writing about her life in 1853. *Incidents* covers major events in Brent's[14] life during her years as a slave in the South and a fugitive in the North, including her attempts to rebuff and put an end to the incessant sexual advances of her de facto owner, Dr. Flint, as well as to avoid the emotional and physical cruelty of Dr. Flint's jealous wife; it also details her struggles to free her two children. The text ends in what Brent considers the self-contradictory moment at which her freedom is purchased by the northern white woman by whom she was employed.[15]

Incidents is explicitly addressed to northern whites, particularly northern white Christian women.[16] And it is in many ways quite self-conscious about its aims: as mentioned earlier, Brent explicitly says that she hopes to "kindle a flame of compassion in [northern] hearts for my sisters who are still in bondage, suffering as I once suffered," in such a way that readers will join those "laboring to advance the cause of humanity" (29–30), that is, join the abolitionist movement.[17] Well aware that most northerners were ignorant, misinformed, or simply complacent about the meaning of slavery for slaves themselves, Brent wanted to provide the kind of information that would generate the sort of feeling likely to lead to action on behalf of slaves.

Linda Brent's anxiety about the extent of the members of her audience's knowledge of events in her life, and the accuracy of their interpretation of her experience, is expressed throughout the text. Sometimes she worries that they can't possibly know what slavery is like ("You never knew what it is to be a slave" [55; see also 141, 173]).[18] At other times she insists that surely the mothers in particular in her audience can know what it is like to have their children torn from them (16, 23). *Incidents* is a sustained attempt to give shape to and control the meaning of the compassion of its white audience. Brent wishes to contribute to determinations of what the actual harms of slavery are and what, in considerable detail, ought to be the response to such harms. In this way she is hoping to highlight the insidious political dynamics of caring for the downtrodden about which Grimké, Harper, Arendt, and others were so concerned: feeling for others in their suffering can simply be a way of asserting authority over them to the extent that such feeling leaves no room for them to have a view about what their suffering means, or what the most appropriate response to it is.

Brent, then, was keenly aware of the risks she was taking in pleading for compassion. Her recognition of these risks, and the lengths she went to to counteract them, tell us a lot about the moral and political dangers of becoming the object of compassion. In many ways *Incidents* is a lesson in how to assert your status as moral agent, and maintain authorship of your experiences, even as you urge your audience to focus on the devastating suffering to which you have been subjected against your will. Brent is well aware that in the process of getting her audience to feel for her and other slaves as crushed victims of an evil institution supported by cruel people, she may simply provoke hostile disapproval of her actions and character, or an anemic kindliness, mistakenly understood by those who feel it to be proof of their Christian virtue. So she takes great care *instructing* her audience about what they are to think and feel: she alerts the members of her audience to the kinds of misreadings and misunderstandings to which they are likely to be subject;

she tries to establish herself as a moral agent and political commentator and not simply a victim; and she encourages her audience to feel not only compassion but outrage in response to slavery.

First, Brent distinguishes the response she is looking for from other responses with which it had been or could be easily confused, especially in the social and political climate of the United States in the mid-nineteenth century. She has only scorn for those alleged forms of affection and generosity not uncommonly exhibited by slave owners for their chattel—for example, treacly memories of "faithful slaves" (7) and yearly gifts of hateful clothing (11). Slaves are so often deceived by whites, Jacobs says, that they have no reason to trust that "kind words" have anything but some "selfish purpose" (169; cf. 158). She sees right through Dr. Flint, whose dealings with her centered around his incessant sexual harassment, and she ridicules his offer of kindly feelings toward her as proof of his forbearance from using all the powers of violence at his disposal. She refuses to regard such feelings as something for which she ought to feel gratitude (59, 61).

In her commentary on the meaning of all these varieties of "kindly feeling," Linda Brent puts her audience on notice: she does not wish to be understood to be asking for feelings in whites that are simply weapons demonstrating their cruel power. She makes clear that the kind of response she is hoping for from northern whites is entirely different from what passes as kindly Christian feeling in the South (12, 31, 124). Even when expressions of charity are not laced with condescension, being the object of charity is hardly to be compared with being the subject of freedom (89, 201).

She does provide instructive examples of the type of feeling she *does* value. She singles out for readers' attention unnamed abolitionists who in the process of inquiring about her life and her escape from slavery indicated recognition of her full membership in the human community by careful concern not to "wound [her] feelings" (161). In expressing admiration and gratitude for the response she got from the abolitionists Amy and Isaac Post, Brent makes no reference to how they feel but rather to how they judged: "They measured a man's worth by his character, not by his complexion" (189).

Indeed, in many ways Brent is much less interested in how friendly people may feel about her and her story than in whether their actions reveal that they take her seriously as a moral agent. I don't say this because I think we ought to dismiss her plea for compassion. There is no doubt that however stylized it was—however much it was the expected and proper mode of politely if urgently drawing attention to her plight—she was dismayed and appalled not only by the absence of such feeling but by the presence of cruelty (see 28) and so certainly welcomed what she sometimes called "womanly sympathy" (162) or deeds of "Christian womanhood" (100). But Brent was not to be satisfied with the simple invocation of the right feeling, and there is much to suggest that Brent herself was well aware of the ironic uses to which such stock images as "[the one] who pities my oppressed people" (201) or "the poor, trembling fugitive" (111) could be put even if she did not always use them ironically.[19] Brent was aware of the need to employ wooden, stereotypical images of the helper and the helped, the savior and the sufferer, even as she did much to complicate and revise the impoverished ideas they invoked.[20]

But going beyond stock imagery was risky, too, for to talk about the particularities of her experience as a slave was to reveal facts about her that she had good reason to believe would not induce compassion, but harsh judgment. Among the horrors and great difficulties of being a slave was engaging in behavior that you might only not like but that you found immoral, that you felt bad about doing even while rightly reckoning that you had little or no control over whether you did it or not. Many if not most slave girls and women were raped or otherwise sexually assaulted or harassed by white boys and men; there was an unwritten law among white and Blacks that this was not to be talked about (28).[21] But as Linda Brent makes clear, it was also painful and risky for slave women to talk about such experiences to white women they implored for help, on account of that cruel logic according to which being subject to sexual assault is first and foremost an indication of the victim's immorality. (Indeed, Brent was reluctant to talk to her own dear grandmother about Dr. Flint, saying she "felt shamefaced about telling her such impure things" [29].) At the same time, part of the case she wishes to make to her white Christian audience about the evils of slavery is that it not only sanctioned and encouraged sexual encounters between white men and Black women but in many ways depended upon them for the continued creation of slave bodies.[22]

Having decided to put herself and other slave women forward as in need of the compassion of white northerners, Brent faced what we might call the dilemma of compassion: she could keep to a minimum the information necessary to invoke compassion, relying on stock images of trembling fugitives and kindly rescuers, and hence risk playing into the master-slave relationship she deplored; or she could reveal herself much further, in hopes of presenting herself as more than a mere victim, but at the risk of incurring hard questions about her behavior. That is, on the one hand she could try to invoke the aid of others without providing much contextual information. But this invites people to think of you only in terms of how you have suffered or been victimized; it risks forfeiting the possibility of establishing other facts about yourself that you don't want your audience to lose sight of, such as how you are not a victim but a moral agent. It obscures your right to question and critically appraise your would-be helper as a moral equal. The extent to which one person imploring the help of another does not dare to criticize the helper is a measure of the extent to which the sufferer is at the mercy of the savior.

In order to avoid the narrow roles of sufferer-savior, you can leap to the other horn of the dilemma and provide the kind of information about your state that will not only adequately inform your helper about important details but also will preclude the helper from seeing you simply as someone to whom horrible things have happened. By presenting yourself as not only in need of great help, but also as someone who makes decisions and judgments, you open up the possibility to your helper that despite your being in great need you are still capable of and insist on the right to make judgments about her even as she helps you. However, this course has serious risks, too: you cannot assume the benefits of being considered such an agent without also being subject to its burdens. The more you reveal about yourself and the more you establish yourself as other than a victim, the more likely you are to be the object of others' harsh judgments—especially if you are a nineteenth-century Black female slave alluding to sexual liaisons.

Linda Brent refers fairly directly to this dilemma when she reports to her white audience about an exchange she had with a particularly helpful abolitionist: Brent "frankly told him some of the most important events of my life. It was painful for me to do it; but I would not deceive him. If he was desirous of being my friend, I thought he ought to know how far I was worthy of it." The gentleman warned her: "Your straight-forward answers do you credit; but don't answer every body so openly. It might give some heartless people a pretext for treating you with contempt" (160).

This is a spectacular move by Brent. While it's true that earlier in the text she lets the members of her audience know that what she has to say may disturb them, here she instructs them about how any decent person would regard her revelations: only heartless people would have contempt for such honesty, would fail to see that Brent must provide authentic information if her would-be helpers are really to understand her situation.[23]

Brent, then, instructs her audience members in what they are to feel by distinguishing the reactions she hopes for from ones that she distrusts, by talking about exemplary responses, and by indicating her recognition of the risks she takes in providing the kind of information that she does.

Second, Brent insists on expressing her status as a moral agent. She sometimes speaks as if much of what slaves do they have to do, they are compelled to do. For example, early in the text, as she subtly introduces her audience to the "foul" (27) and "impure" (29) things white masters talk about or did to their

Black female slaves, she says "she drank the cup of sin, and shame, and misery, whereof her persecuted race are compelled to drink" (29); so powerful are the forces allied against slaves that "resistance is hopeless" (51; cf. 100). And yet *Incidents* celebrates her and other slaves' resistance,[24] even as Brent acknowledges that often in resisting she did things that she regards as "wrong" (55) and for which she cannot and does not wish to "screen [my]self behind the plea of compulsion" (54). In particular she is "haunted" by the "painful and humiliating memory" of entering into a sexual relationship with another white man, in order to get Dr. Flint off her back. But she uses the occasion of bringing up this fact about her life to carve out a moral position somewhere between excusing herself, on the one hand, and presenting herself as unqualifiedly deserving of blame, on the other. She suggests to her audience that there are indeed standards by which she ought to be judged, but perhaps they are *not* those by which free people, free women, are to be judged (56). She takes pains to make clear that she has standards by which she appraises her own actions, even those toward whites: she takes pride in never "wrongirg" or ever wishing to wrong her cruel mistress Mrs. Flint (32); she worries about the harm that may come to those helping her escape, and insists that being caught would be better than "causing an innocent person to suffer kindness to me" (98).

We may be inclined to regard some of this as evidence of her heightened awareness of the need to convince her audience of her moral stature. But that is the point: she doesn't want her plea for help to erase her status as someone who nevertheless has difficult moral dilemmas about which she has had to make painful decisions for which she bears responsibility. For example, she takes responsibility for having made the extremely difficult decision to separate herself from her children in order to try to save them (85, 91, 141). She puts herself forward as a person with moral standards, who wishes to live under conditions in which she can be "a useful woman and a good mother" (133). She is ready to rebuke herself for selfishness (135). If she doesn't want her call for help to erase or exclude her status as someone who has moral standards to live up to, neither does she want it to render her ineligible as a moral critic of whites, southern or northern. For example, she does not hesitate to make sarcastic remarks about Mrs. Flint, her mistress, who prides herself on her Christian charity but enjoys inflicting mental and physical pain on Brent and other slaves (12, 13, 124, 136), even while pretending to be moved by their sorrows (124, 146). Mrs. Flint well knows her husband's ways, but instead of helping her female slaves respond to them, she simply inflicts her rage on the women (310). Like many other slave owners' wives, Mrs. Flint uses cruelty toward slaves to establish authority over them (92).

And yet just as she has wondered aloud about the extent to which slavery forces slaves into morally compromising dilemmas, so Brent has an eye for the moral damage slavery does to whites (52): "slavery is a curse to the whites as well as to the blacks. It makes the white fathers cruel and sensual; the sons violent and licentious; it contaminates the daughters, and makes the wives wretched. . . . Yet few slaveholders seem to be aware of the widespread moral ruin occasioned by this wicked system. Their talk is of blighted cotton crops—not of the blight on their children's souls."(52)

In remarking that "cruelty is contagious in uncivilized communities" (47; cf. 198, 200), Brent wonders just how "civilized" slave-owning society can be. Slavery "pervert[s] all the natural feelings of the human heart" (142). The power it affords poor whites prevents them from seeing how it in fact keeps them in "poverty, ignorance, and moral degradation" (64).

Brent thus establishes herself in the moral community in a variety of ways. She expresses worry about what she takes to be immoral acts that slavery pushed slaves to commit. She presents herself as subject to moral standards. But she also exercises the right to contribute to an examination of what those standards ought to be, not only by introducing the possibility that people living under slavery ought not to be held to *all* the same standards as free people, but also by frequently offering biting critiques of the character and actions of southern and northern whites.

Third, while there is no doubt that Linda Brent values and hopes to succeed in prompting compassion from her audience, she also frequently suggests, directly or indirectly, that outrage would be an appropriate response to the conditions under which slaves (and fugitives) live. For example, early in the text she describes a scene that at first might strike the reader as a somewhat stylized attempt to pull the heartstrings, particularly those of the mothers in her audience: "Could you have seen that mother clinging to her child, when they fastened the irons upon his wrists; could you have heard her heart-rending groans, and seen her blood-shot eyes wander wildly from face to face, vainly pleading for mercy" (23). "Could you have seen this . . . ," then what? You would have been moved to tears? You would have felt for the mother, and stretched out a helping hand? That is not what Brent says: "could you have witnessed that scene as I saw it, you would exclaim, *Slavery is damnable!*" (23; emphasis in original).

Brent does not hesitate to express scorn for white northerners—especially "doctors of divinity" who make quick trips to the South, allow themselves to be hoodwinked, wined, dined, and flattered by their slaveholding hosts, and return North to chastise abolitionists. About such a "revered gentleman" she comments: "What does *he* know of the half-starved wretches toiling from dawn till dark on the plantations? of mothers shrieking for their children, torn from their arms by slave traders? of young girls dragged down into moral filth? of pools of blood around the whipping post? of hounds trained to tear human flesh? of men screwed into cotton gins to die? The slaveholder showed him none of these things, and the slaves dared not tell of them if he had asked them" (74; emphasis in original). Such a description does not seem intended so much to promote compassion for slaves as to evoke outrage at slave owners and the northerners who are duped by them. Brent's tone here is much different than when she refers to a slave mother wringing her hands in anguish (16), or describes herself as "one of God's most powerless creatures" (19), or expresses her fervent desire that her daughter "might never feel the weight of slavery's chain" (79). While these latter phrases leave room for, indeed seem to encourage a kind of weepy sadness (shades of *Uncle Tom's Cabin*), the former refer to conditions too horrible, too mean, too painful, too degrading, to be met with feelings as tender as compassion. Even more to the point, compassion in this context would direct us to slaves, while anger and outrage direct us to the slave owners and those who abet them.

In a passage somewhat similar to the above, Brent compares her own situation to that of most other slaves: "I was never cruelly over-worked; I was never lacerated with the whip from head to foot; I was never so beaten and bruised that I could not turn from one side to the other; I never had my heel-strings cut to prevent my running away; I was never chained to a log and forced to drag it about, while I toiled in the fields from morning till night; I was never branded with hot iron, or torn by bloodhounds" (114–115). While it is true that she concludes this description with the comment "God pity the woman who is compelled to lead such a life!" (115) this inventory of slavery's wrongs is calculated, I suggest, to evoke much more than pity or compassion.[25] These are unspeakable horrors, and hearing about them in this way directs attention not so much to those who had to endure them as to the people and the institutions that are responsible for them.

These renderings of the conditions of slavery, geared more to the generation of outrage than compassion, are of a piece with Brent's searing critique of white society. So, even when her description of slavery is not painfully lurid, it is clear that she is not so much concerned about her audience's response to slaves as its response to those who sustain slavery: "Yet that intelligent, enterprising and noble-hearted man was a chattel, liable, by the laws of a country that calls itself civilized, to be sold with horses and pigs!" (156; see also 184, 191).

In assuming the task of providing information about slavery to her audience that will instill outrage and sustained indignation about such things taking place in their country, Brent is further instructing her audience about how it ought to feel. Here she seems to be resisting (self-consciously or not) two fairly strong forces current in the society. (1) Although appealing to the compassion of white northern women played to a virtue that, according to a powerful stereotype for women of their class, religion, and "race,"[26] they were supposed to have and cultivate, appealing to their sense of outrage did not (for example, Angelina Grimké battled with Catharine Beecher over white women's proper role in ending slavery, and their differences in turn reflected a larger battle within abolitionist circles and between abolitionists and non- or anti-abolitionists about the shape and goal of antislavery action).[27] (2) Slave narratives and other abolitionist literature had a very wide readership, but at least some of those readers seemed to find pleasure in the kinds of depictions of cruelty and pain of which we've just seen examples. For such readers some of the narratives were what Robin Winks has referred to as "pious pornography."[28] Lydia Maria Child, who edited *Incidents*, perhaps was referring to such tastes in her comment on rearranging some of Jacobs's manuscript: "I put the savage cruelties into one chapter . . . in order that those who shrink from 'supping upon horrors' might omit them, without interrupting the thread of the story."[29]

Describing slave experience in such a way as to provoke outrage thus could expand some readers' emotional responses even as it checked those of others. Those comfortable in their role as agents of care and compassion might think about whether reluctance to become angry or indignant was keeping them from some kinds of political action. Those finding delight in the revelation of cruelty might find obstacles to their pleasure in hearing moral outrage, not simple pleas for mercy, in the voices of those on whom the cruelty is inflicted.

Linda Brent was highly attuned to the political logic of the variety of emotions her account of slavery was likely to stir up. Knowing the risks she was taking, at every turn she did what she could to minimize the dangers, instructing her readers about the differences among "kindly" responses and about the special moral burdens slavery placed on both slave and slave owner. Instead of allowing her plea for compassion to become an invitation to her audience to take pride in its good feelings, or to demean her as a helpless victim, she uses it as an occasion to exhibit the significance of the slave as moral agent and social critic. And yet she never for a moment suggests that she and other slaves do not need (though they should not "make capital out of"[30]) the good feelings of the very audience receiving lessons from her about what those feelings ought to be.

COMPASSION AND POLITICS

Let us recall Hannah Arendt's worries about attempts to mix compassion and politics. The phenomenon she refers to as compassion is, she insists, by its very nature non- or antipolitical: when one is stricken by, indeed virtually stricken with, the suffering of another, there is not the plurality of subjects, the plurality of perspectives, or the need for speech definitive of political life. Since there is no reason for speech, presenting oneself as compassionate is highly suspect, especially if one attempts to excel or shine at such feeling. When pity parades as compassion and is touted as proof of one's political virtue, the actual needs of particular suffering people are lost in scandalous posturing.

Linda Brent would agree with Arendt's warning about the high stakes involved when some people try to capitalize on other people's suffering. That seems to be why at the very moment of pleading for compassion for herself and other slaves, in effect she offers a disquisition about the difference between real compassion and its insidious imitators, about the ways in which moral agency is not necessarily erased but sometimes acutely enlivened by the unceasing corrosion of slavery. She is responding to the fact that there are any number of possible and actual perspectives on the meaning of the suffering of slaves, including the view that Black slaves are not capable of feeling the kind of pain to which whites are subject.[31] She is announcing her entry into the explicit and implicit battles over what her suffering and the suffering of other slaves means—to them, to whites, to the country, to God.[32]

Brent thus sees suffering as much more deeply political, in Arendtian terms, than Arendt herself does. After all, for Arendt what enables something to become part of the public realm is not whether it can be seen or touched, but whether it can be talked about from a variety of perspectives. The phenomenon Arendt refers to as compassion amounts to a sharing of suffering, not an exchange of views about it. And the only emotional alternative to such compassion is pity, which, as she describes it, is not so much another perspective on pain as a glomming onto it, an unquenchable thirst for the suffering of others, too passionate a pleasure to brook the challenge of any other perspective, especially from the sufferer herself. While Arendt applauds what she calls "solidarity" as a way that nonsufferers "establish deliberately and, as it were, dispassionately a community of interest with the oppressed and exploited," such solidarity "may be aroused by suffering [but] is not guided by it."[33] Solidarity focuses on what nonsufferers and sufferers have in common—for example, their shared humanity or dignity—not on the conditions of want, deprivation, misery, or humiliation which distinguishes them.[34] Nor is suffering the focus of the robust discussions of political life, the deliberations for which a plurality of perspectives is crucial. Arendt strongly implies that there is no need to deliberate over the existence or significance of suffering; if people are hungry you feed them, if they are without shelter you house them. The only question is whether the technological means are there to do it.[35]

In short, Arendt doesn't treat pain and suffering as matters on which there will be a variety of perspectives, topics for the "discussions, deliberations, [and] decisions" of those engaged in "public business" (*OR*, 119). In trying to lead her audience to understand what the right feelings are about the suffering entailed by slavery, Brent seems to be deeply engaged in just the kind of persuasive speech characteristic of Arendt's political domain. For Brent, her freedom, the freedom of other slaves, and the moral health of the nation hinges on her audience finding the right perspective on slaves' experience of suffering, which is why, while she is asking for compassion, she also provides a treatise on its meaning.

What Brent thinks of as compassion is neither what Arendt

calls compassion nor what she calls pity. In asking for the compassion of her audience, Brent seems not at all to want a perspectiveless cofeeling—two people, feeling so much the same thing that it is as if they are one—but informed passion from someone who is without doubt another subject, occupying quite a different position. Brent agrees with Arendt that the gap between nonsufferer and sufferer should not be bridged by a self-congratulatory, virtue-attesting pity; but she doesn't believe or hope that there will be a collapse of the difference between nonsufferer and sufferer. Brent doesn't insist that others be stricken with her pain, only that they come to understand it properly and be inclined to act accordingly. Her plea for compassion in the context of accompanying instruction suggests that she regards compassion as involving cognition—the compassionate person sees the sufferer under a particular description—but nevertheless having a kind of cognitive slack or cognitive recklessness, inasmuch as that description may stand in need of correction and adjustment. Unlike Arendt, Brent assumes what has come to be called a "cognitivist" view about the nature of emotion—certainly about the nature of compassion.[36] She seems to believe that feeling responses to others' pain can stand in need of and thus must be formatted for fine tuning. Unlike Arendt, whose strict distinction of passion from reason seems to entail that compassion as a passion is incapable of adjustment, Brent treats compassion as capable of being informed by knowledge and hence capable of change, of enlightenment.

Indeed, as Ronald Hepburn has argued, it is precisely this feature of our emotions (or at least of some of them) that makes us responsive to and educated by good literature.[37] The more carefully a situation is delineated, the more particularized the emotional response it brings forth; and the more thoughtfully an emotional response is rendered, the more closely depicted the situation to which it is a response. Hepburn says, for example, that in *Anna Karenina* Tolstoy expands the reader's emotional repertoire when Levin's new child is described in such a way that we understand why he feels not what "greeting-card emotion-stereotypes" would have us expect, but apprehension. Simultaneously, in order to understand the presence of such emotion, we have to think about aspects of the child and its birth that are the objects of the fear. While a lesser writer might simply have employed stock imagery and drawn a clichéd association between a child's birth and a father's joy, Tolstoy shows us ways in which emotional responses can be and are more complicated and less predictable.

Brent, as we have seen, is not unwilling to employ stock images of anguished mothers and trembling fugitives, but *Incidents* as a whole provides a context in which the audience can correct and expand the naive, stereotyped emotional response such imagery calls forth. *Incidents* pleads for the audience's compassion, but describes in considerable detail the persons for whom such compassion is to be felt. We are to understand that such persons themselves have complicated reactions to the suffering they have had to undergo. For example, what is it about slavery that is most painful? For Linda Brent's brother William, it was not "the smart of the whip," but "the *idea* of being whipped" (19; emphasis in original); for Brent it was particularly galling that as a "favorite slave" she was "not allowed to have any pride of character" (31); she took on a white male lover rather than bow to Dr. Flint's importuning because she found it "less degrading to give one's self, than to submit to compulsion" (55). We are to understand that such persons are not necessarily so brutalized by the conditions under which they live (or—though Jacobs will not stoop to even mention the possibility—so "naturally" brutal) that they have ceased to regard themselves as moral agents who bear the burdens and enjoy the rights pertaining thereto (being subject to moral standards themselves; evaluating the behavior of both slave owners and slaves as they see fit).

Arendt doesn't think there is anything to be gained, and in fact much to be lost, when discussions about suffering take place. But Brent assumes that compassion typically must become fine-tuned through a process of exchange between the nonsufferer and the sufferer in which the nonsufferer's passion is honed by growing awareness of the details of the sufferer's being and situation. Brent recognizes the relation between what one sees (or allows oneself to see) and what one feels in a number of ways: in her awareness of the difference between depicting suffering in order to generate compassion and depicting it in order to encourage outrage; in her insistence that if northern "doctors of divinity . . . felt the interest in the poor and the lowly, that they ought to feel, they would not be so *easily* blinded" (73; emphasis in original).

Thus while Arendt and Brent share many worries about the political abuses to which compassion and its close emotional relatives are susceptible, there are important and illuminating differences between them. Arendt thinks that the only way to avoid such abuses is to rule out contest over the meaning of pain and suffering as part of political life, which she tries to effect in part by insisting that the only honorable emotional response to the suffering of others is a perspectiveless cosuffering. Brent, however, assumes that contest over the meaning of pain and suffering of slaves is central to the moral and political life around her and that the way to avoid the risks yet enjoy the benefits of becoming the object of compassion is to try to add her voice to that debate.

Thus, while Arendt's work is particularly helpful in describing some of the abuses to which suffering is subject in the hands of those proclaiming their feelings for sufferers, Jacobs successfully shows how protecting compassion from such abuse does not require the strong medicine Arendt prescribes in trying to cabin it off completely from political life. The solution is not to prohibit discussions of the meaning of the suffering of particular people, but, if possible, to make sure that those who are suffering participate in the discussion—which means acknowledging their status as moral and political agents even as one recognizes and responds to their condition of suffering. The presence of such discussions doesn't mean that the participants somehow have left the world of emotion. Such discussions and debates remind us that our emotional lives often are highly politicized—for example, when we struggle over whose pain counts, what such pain means, and who gets to provide answers to those questions.

Compassion, like so many of our other complex emotions, has a heady political life. Invoking compassion is an important means of trying to direct social, political, and economic resources in one's direction (indeed, compassion is one of those resources). Existing inequalities between persons may be exacerbated rather than reduced through the expression of compassion. Interpretive battles over the significance of a person's or a group's suffering reflect larger political battles over the right to legislate meaning. The political stakes in the definition, evaluation, and distribution of compassion are very high.[38]

Chapter Four

THE VIRTUE OF FEELING
AND THE FEELING OF VIRTUE

The mother who taught me what I know
of tenderness and love and compassion
taught me also the bleak rituals of keeping
Negroes in their place.

—Lillian Smith[1]

A *theme at the center of chapter 2*
has made an otherwise rather quiet appearance in these pages
so far: how does focusing on sufferers in particular ways highlight or obscure the role of the agents thought to be responsible
for that suffering?[2] We saw that part of what so exercised Plato
about Homer and the tragedians was that, in his view, they
wrongly tended to blame the gods for the great trials and tribulations to which humans are subject. When we looked closely at
the way the notion of slavery as "the American tragedy" directs
our attention to the suffering of slaves, we saw that it tends to
makes the failings of the agents responsible for such suffering
more interesting than the responses of those who suffer.

Harriet Jacobs wanted both to bring proper attention to the
condition of slaves and to make sure her audience also paid at-

tention to those who maintained slavery. So, in the voice of Linda Brent, she tried to generate outrage at their deeds and alarm at the moral state of their souls. Moreover, given Brent's sharp criticisms of the cruel Mrs. Flint, and her refusal to give up the right to criticize northerners even as she asked for their help, we should not forget that among those she holds responsible for the suffering of slaves is other women. Indeed, we would be suspiciously selective if, in our admiration for her spunkiness as a slave woman who insisted that she not be seen simply as a victim, we manage to ignore the fact that she attests to the history of the cruelty and inhumanity of some women toward others. Just as Brent insisted that her status as slave not be used to excuse her from some degree of responsibility for her actions, so she insisted implicitly that Mrs. Flint's status as wife of a cruel and wily man not be used to excuse her from some degree of responsibility for her treatment of Brent and other slaves. We would be doing some interesting picking and choosing if, from the story of Linda Brent, we decided not to pay any attention to its depiction of the cruelties inflicted by women on women.

Moreover, it is not as if Mrs. Flint's treatment of Linda Brent is an anomaly in the history of women's relationships with one another. The history of women, including the history of feminism and feminists, is hardly free of some women doing violence to others, of some women miserably failing other women in need. For example, as is well documented, nineteenth-century white middle-class suffragists were ready and willing to use racist arguments in the name of advancing what they called "women's interests."[3] Some white women routinely beat Black women who were their slaves.[4] Nazi women gave their all in the effort to eliminate the Jewish population of Europe—which in-

cluded, of course, Jewish women.⁵ Women who demand the
strictest scrutiny of the conditions under which they work and
of the fairness of their salaries don't necessarily show the same
concern for the working conditions of the women who take care
of their children or clean their condos.⁶

I do not wish to suggest here that some women have a
monopoly on the mistreatment of other women; and by using
these examples rather than others I run the risk of making the
sins of some women just more important than those of others⁷
and thus the risk of simply reasserting the privileged position
of some women in Western feminism. But there are far too few
sustained examinations of women's oppression or exploitation
of other women.⁸ As Berenice Fisher once put it, when commenting on the growing use of "guilt" at feminist conferences:
"although we frequently employed the language of 'guilt,' virtually no one paid attention to guilt as a moral issue, that is, to the
realities of wrongdoing and the responsibilities and consequences entailed by it."⁹ I want to offer a few reasons for this virtual silence and then suggest a way we might explore some of
the moral dimensions of women's treatment and mistreatment
of one another.

CARING FOR WHOM?

Why has the question of women's treatment of one another not
been a burning issue for much of feminism? First of all, one
of the stereotypes about themselves many women have had to

battle is the image that we are catty and callous toward one another, really only interested in men and their money, their prestige, their bodies, or, in some cases, all of these. So perhaps it has seemed hard to make a publicly understandable feminist case about the oppression of women without simultaneously remaining mute on the topic of some women's oppression of or plain meanness toward other women. According to this way of thinking, it is, to begin with, too difficult psychologically to talk about oneself or other women as both victim and victimizer. For example, perhaps it is not easy to feel sympathy for the abused wives of white slave owners and at the same time be critical of some of their actions toward their female (and male) slaves. Moreover, under such circumstances it is inviting to lay the blame for our own or others' shortcomings at the feet of those who have victimized us or them. But however we might explain the reluctance or caution about discussing women's bad treatment of other women, taking those groups of women seriously requires that we do just that.

There aren't only psychological motives for shying away from examination of women's mistreatment of one another. Many of the tools of feminist thinking work against the possiblity that those of us who are feminists will consider it an important theoretical or practical concern to investigate the absence of care or the presence of hostility, hatred, and contempt among women.

First of all, until recently many of us feminists have done little to shake a habit we share with many of our fellow citizens: talking loosely about "men and women," as if the men and women had no racial, class, or cultural identity; talking about "women and Blacks," or "women and minorities," as if there were no Black women, or no women in the groups called "minorities"; comparing relations between "men and women" to those between "whites and Blacks" or "rich and poor" or "colonizer and colonized," which precludes us from talking about differences between women—between white and Black women, or rich and poor, or colonizer and colonized. In addition, much feminist theory and history is filled with incessant comparisons between "women" on the one hand and "Blacks," the "poor," "Jews," and so forth, on the other. For example, consider the talk about women being treated like slaves. Whenever we talk that way we are not only making clear that the "women" we're referring to aren't themselves slaves; we're making it impossible to talk about how the women who weren't slaves treated those who were.

Until we were encouraged to talk about differences among women, it remained hard to talk about how women treat one another. Moreover, the effort by some feminists to delineate an "ethics of care,"[10] as well as the struggle to enable the role of emotions in human life to be taken seriously, paradoxically (but perhaps not so accidentally) has diverted our attention from the history of the lack of care of women for women. Some passages from Jane Austen's *Emma* illustrate what I have in mind.

Emma, our lively young protagonist, is deep into a debate with Mr. George Knightley about the behavior of Frank Churchill. Young Churchill did not grow up with his father and stepmother, who are part of Emma's and Knightley's social circle. A visit by Churchill to his father and stepmother has been long awaited. Emma and Knightley disagree in their assessment of Churchill's delay in making the trip:

KNIGHTLEY: *"I cannot believe that he has not the power of coming, if he made a point of it. It is too unlikely for me to believe it without proof.... If Frank Churchill had wanted to see his father, he would have contrived it between September and January. A man at his age—what is he? three or four-and-twenty—cannot be without the means of doing as much as that. It is impossible."*

EMMA: *"You are the worst judge in the world, Mr. Knightley, of the difficulties of dependence. You do not know what it is to have tempers to manage.... It is very unfair to judge of anybody's conduct without an intimate knowledge of their situation. Nobody, who has not been in the interior of a family, can say what the difficulties of any individual of that family may be."*

KNIGHTLEY: *"There is one thing, Emma, which a man can always do, if he chooses, and that is, his duty.... It is Frank Churchill's duty to pay this attention to his father."*

EMMA: *"You have not an idea of what is requisite in situations directly opposite to your own.... I can imagine that if you, as you are ... were to be transported and placed all at once in Mr. Frank Churchill's situation, you would be able to say and do just what you have been recommending for him; and it might have a very good effect ... but then you would have no habits of early obedience and long observance to break through. To him who has, it might not be so easy to burst*

> *forth at once into perfect independence.... Oh, the differ-*
> *ence of situation and habit! I wish you would try to un-*
> *derstand what an amiable young man may be likely to feel*
> *in directly opposing [the other adults who had brought him*
> *up].*"

KNIGHTLEY: "*Your amiable young man is a very weak young*
man, if this be the first occasion of his carrying through a reso-
lution to do right against the will of others. It ought to have
been a habit with him, by this time, of following his duty, in-
stead of consulting expediency."

EMMA: "*We are both prejudiced! you against, I for him; and we*
have no chance of agreeing till he is really here."

KNIGHTLEY: "*Prejudiced! I am not prejudiced.*"

EMMA: "*But I am very much, and without being at all ashamed*
of it. My love for [his father and stepmother] gives me a de-
cided prejudice in his favour."[11]

I think anyone interested in the work of Carol Gilligan and
those influenced by her work would find the contrasts between
Knightley's and Emma's judgments about Frank Churchill to
be, at least on their face, illustrative of two conceptions of morality that seem to be quite distinct.[12]

Knightley's concern for principled behavior, impartial judgment, and everyone's getting their due seems to exemplify an
"ethics of justice" (said to be more likely to be held by men
than women). For Knightley there are at least two principles
that ought to be brought to bear: the duty Churchill has to his
father, and the importance of Knightley himself remaining un-
biased in his judgment of Churchill. Whatever relationship

Churchill has to his more immediate family can't be as important as his duty to his own father; whatever the particular facts of the circumstances Churchill finds himself in cannot be used by Churchill, or by anyone else, to mitigate the full weight of his duty.

Emma's insistence on the contextual details of the situation, and her concern for the importance of the many relationships involved (Churchill and his immediate family, Churchill and his father and stepmother, Emma and Churchill, Emma and Knightley), seem characteristic of an "ethics of care" (said more likely to be held by women than men). For Emma, Churchill's formal duty is irrelevant. And Emma's relationship to both Churchill and his father cannot be erased by a formal obligation that she might be said to have to remain "unprejudiced." Knightley's principled judgment of Churchill is not well grounded: he doesn't know enough about what Churchill is capable of, or about the crucial details of Churchill's relationship to his immediate family.

I do not here wish to enter into the ongoing and very rich conversation about such apparently contrasting ethical orientations.[13] Instead, I feel obliged to point out what readers may miss about Emma if they are interested in her only to the degree that her words and actions illustrate an ethics of care in contrast to an ethics of justice.

In the chapter immediately following the one in which we overhear the animated discussion between Emma and Knightley, Emma and her friend Harriet are out for a walk. Austen invites us to eavesdrop again, this time on Emma's private thoughts:

> *They were just approaching the house where lived Mrs. and Miss Bates. . . . There was always sufficient reason for [calling upon them]; Mrs. and Miss Bates loved to be called on; and [Emma] knew she was considered by the very few who presumed ever to see imperfection in her, as rather negligent in that respect, and as not contributing what she ought to the stock of their scanty comforts.*
>
> *She had had many a hint from Mr. Knightley, and some from her own heart, as to her deficiency, but none were equal to counteract the persuasion of its being very disagreeable—a waste of time—tiresome women—and all the horror of being in danger of falling in with the second and third rate of Highbury, who were calling on them for ever, and therefore she seldom went near them.*[14]

If we get thoroughly caught up in comparing Emma's unapologetically biased, particularized caring for Frank Churchill, to Knightley's rather stern, impersonal, principled response, we may fail to ask an important question: for whom does Emma care? What kind of treatment does she give those she regards as her social and economic inferiors? The fact—if it is one—that some women, in reflections on their moral problems, show care, and a fine sense of complexity appreciative of context, tells us nothing about who they think worthy of their care, nor whose situation demands attention to details and whose does not.

Moreover, as I discussed in chapter 3, there are forms of care that are not only compatible with but in some contexts crucial to the maintenance of systematic inequalities among women. In *Between Women: Domestics and Their Employers*, Judith Rollins describes in some detail the maternalism expressed by some white female employers toward their Black female domestic employees:

> *The maternalism dynamic is based on the assumption of a superordinate-subordinate relationship. While maternalism may protect and nurture, it also degrades and insults. The "caring" that is expressed in maternalism might range from an adult-to-child to a human-to-pet kind of caring but, by definition (and by the evidence presented by my data), it is not human-to-equal-human caring. The female employer, with her motherliness and protectiveness and generosity, is expressing in a distinctly feminine way her lack of respect for the domestic as an autonomous, adult employee. While the female employer typically creates a more intimate relationship with a domestic than her male counterpart does, this should not be interpreted as meaning she values the human worth of the domestic any more highly than does the more impersonal male employer.*[15]

Feminist interest in exploring an ethics of care and the closely related emphasis on the importance of emotions in our lives paradoxically has encouraged us to ignore the absence of care by women for other women, to disregard the presence of "negative" emotional reactions by women to other women. I now want to make this claim more specific by focusing on the ways in which our emotions reveal the moral dimensions of our relationships—in particular, how our emotions reveal how seriously we take the concerns of others, what we take to be our responsibility for others' plights, and the extent to which we regard others as even having points of view we need to take seriously.

EMOTION AND RESPONSIBILITY

Our emotions, or at least some of them, can be highly revelatory of whom and what we care or don't care about. These emotions provide powerful clues to the ways in which we take ourselves to be implicated in the lives of others and they in ours. As the following example from Aristotle reveals, many of our emotions locate us in moral relation to one another: one who doesn't get angry when the occasion calls for it "is thought not to feel things nor to be pained by them, and since he does not get angry, he is thought unlikely to defend himself; and to endure being insulted, and put up with insult to one's friends, is slavish" (*Nicomachean Ethics* 1126a6–8).

Aristotle insists here that if under certain conditions we don't feel anger, we may have failed to show proper respect for ourselves or proper concern for our friends.

Another example of the relation between our emotional and moral lives has to do with the blatant displays of racism at many educational institutions in the United States. For instance, consider the messages, left by cowards in protective anonymity, telling African American, Latina, and Chinese American students in no uncertain terms that they don't belong at the college and that if they don't like the way they're treated they should "go home." (These represent only the obvious tip of an iceberg, melting with what the Supreme Court in a related context called "all deliberate speed.") I do not wish to go into the details here of how any particular institution actually has responded to what, in a revealing phrase, typically are called "incidents" (a term that suggests, perhaps insists, that such events are infrequent and anomalous). But, by way of beginning to show what our emotions tell us about our moral relations to one another, and the contours and quality of our care for one another, I'd like to run through some possible responses.

1. Ivylawn College regrets the occurrence of racist incidents on its campus.
2. Ivylawn College is embarrassed by the occurrence of racist incidents on its campus.
3. Ivylawn College feels guilty about the occurrence of racist incidents on its campus.
4. Ivylawn College feels shame for the occurrence of racist incidents on its campus.[16]

Surely you already notice some significant difference between regret, embarrassment, guilt, and shame. Think also of the difference between these two:

5. Ivylawn College regrets the occurrence of racist incidents on its campus.
6. Ivylawn College regrets the harm done to those hurt by the recent events on its campus.

If the first set of contrasts reminds us that different emotions imply varying notions of responsibility and depth of concern, the second reminds us that the same emotion can have different objects—what the emotions are about. In exploring these emotions in more detail, I turn to Gabriele Taylor's *Pride, Shame, and Guilt: Emotions of Self-Assessment.*[17]

Gabriele Taylor is one of a number of contemporary philosophers who operate on the basis of what has been dubbed the cognitive theory of the emotions. Though cognitivists differ on certain details, they share the conviction that emotions cannot simply be feelings, like churnings in our stomachs, fluttering of hearts, chokings in our throats. Such feelings may accompany my regretting having hurt you, or my sense of shame in having hurt you, but the difference between my regret and my shame cannot be accounted for by reference to such feelings; nor can the difference between my regret in having hurt *you* and my regret in having hurt *my father*. There is a kind of logic to our emotions that has nothing to do with whatever mute feelings may accompany them (in many cases there don't even seem to be such feelings).

The central tenet of what is currently known as the cognitive theory of emotions is that our emotions are not a clue to or sign of internal poppings and firings and other gyrations—mental or physical—within us, but rather indicate how we see the world. Typically emotions have identificatory cognitive states: what identifies my emotion as anger is, among other things, a belief that some unjust harm has been done; what makes my emotion a matter of fear is, among other things, my belief that danger is imminent. I shall not go into more detail about the cognitive theory here, but it is perhaps worth making explicit that we could not regard our emotions as very interesting facts about us—in particular, as deeply connected to ourselves as moral agents—if emotions were simply internal events, things happening in us like headaches or bleeding gums.[18]

That said, let us return to our earlier examples of regret, embarrassment, guilt, and shame. As Taylor reminds us, if I regret that something happened, then I must regard what happened as in some sense undesirable. But I need not regard what happened as anything morally troubling—for example, I may regret not taking a few more days of vacation; and I can feel regret for something for which I was in no way responsible (Taylor's example is the passing of summer.)[19] Moreover, even though regretting that an event happened means I must take it to be in some sense undesirable, it is still possible for me to think that nevertheless, all things considered, it is not something I think should not have happened. And it is perfectly possible for me to regret it without being at all inclined to take any action in consequence. This is why we can perfectly sincerely send our regrets—indeed, even our "deepest regrets"—that a party occurs on a night when we're out of town. It might have been fun to go to the party, and I might be a bit apprehensive about hurting the feelings of or disappointing a good friend, but it is more important to do what takes me out of town and I don't want my friend to change the date of the party.

In all these ways, Taylor points out, regret is quite different from remorse. You can't feel remorse about something for which you do not believe yourself to be responsible; nor about something that doesn't appear to you to be morally wrong; nor about something you don't wish to undo or attend to in some way.

So if Ivylawn College expresses regret that what it calls a "racist incident" happened on its campus, all the college is doing so far is acknowledging that such an event took place and allowing that that was in some unspecified sense undesirable. But it is not in any way assuming responsibility for the "incident," nor indicating that there is anything morally troubling about it—as opposed to its just being undesirable for its nuisance value in terms of college publicity—nor indicating that any action is in consequence required. Notice that because regret has these features, there are certain built-in limitations on the description of what is regretted: while it is perfectly possible to regret something described as a "racist incident," I'm sure no institution would publicly say that it regretted the murder of one student by another.

Having sketched out what the presence of regret means, we can keep on the back burner what its absence means—the lack of acknowledgement that anything of note happened at all, let alone that it was in some way undesirable.

I shall then, without regret, move on to embarrassment. My guess is that most educational institutions are embarrassed by the occurrence of racism on their campuses, but they would not describe themselves in just that way. The reasons for this will become clear as we look at the logic of embarrassment (here again with Taylor's help). Embarrassment, unlike regret, necessarily involves a sense that one has been exposed, and consequently is subject to an adverse judgment of oneself in some respect. Suppose a man is embarrassed about beating his wife. His being embarrassed is fully compatible with his finding nothing wrong in the fact that he beats his wife. For his adverse judgment of himself has to do with his not yet quite knowing how to respond to the audience to whom he is or imagines himself exposed, and does not have to do with acting in a way he thinks wrong. If all he feels is embarrassed, he doesn't need to do any basic repair work on himself but only figure out how to deal with the audience—perhaps tell them it is none of their business, or insist that women need to be pushed around, or laugh it off. Perhaps he'll express regret that it is necessary to beat his wife in order to keep her in her place (so the expression of regret might cancel embarrassment). His concern is not about what he is doing to his wife but about the kind of impression he is making on others.

What, then, does it mean if Ivylawn College is embarrassed by the racist incidents on its campus—and why might it or other institutions be unlikely to publicly describe itself in this way? If an institution is embarrassed by the occurrence of racist remarks and other behavior, then what it finds troubling is not the behavior itself, but the exposure of the behavior. If there is anything wrong with the institution, it is that it does not know how to prevent adverse publicity or deal well with it once such public notice is present. When an institution is embarrassed, and only embarrassed, it puts its public relations department to work; it focuses not on changing the institution but on changing the public's perception of the institution. Admitting to embarrassment is usually not a good way of dealing with embarrassment, for it simply brings attention to the situation that the embarrassed party does not want others to see.

You can feel embarrassed without thinking that you have done anything wrong, or something you think you shouldn't do, but in general[20] you can't feel guilty without believing that you have failed to live up to some kind of standard or that you have done something that, according to an accepted authority (including your conscience), is forbidden. (Of course you can be guilty without feeling guilty, but here we are talking only about the latter.) There is something I have done or failed to do, but, according to Taylor, though in feeling guilt I certainly am judging myself adversely, I do not think my situation is hopeless or that I am less of a person than I thought I was. I simply did something I think I shouldn't have or failed to do something I think I ought to have done. There is a blot on my record, but then these blots are only against the background of an otherwise still morally intact person and there are things I can do to repair the damage I've done. Indeed, the action I take is geared to restoring the blot-free picture of myself—so, Taylor insists, if I feel guilty about harming someone else, the thought is not so much that "I have harmed *her*" but rather "*I* have harmed her" (92) and hence disfigured myself to some extent. In response, I may want to do something about the harm I did to her, but—to the extent that my concern is more about myself than about her—as a means of restoring my status in my own eyes.

Taylor's analysis, then, implies that the man who beats his wife and feels guilty about it, unlike the man who merely feels embarrassed, does believe that he has done something he ought not to do, and feeling this way he is inclined to take action to alleviate the feeling. But his concern is not directly for his wife but for himself. If her pain is the occasion for his thinking he has violated something he stands for, his ceasing to beat her, or his otherwise atoning for what he has done, is the means to his self-rehabilitation.

Could Ivylawn College feel guilty about the racism on its campus? Of course this sounds odd in a way that ascribing regret to the institution does not. Feeling guilty involves a sense of direct responsibility for the deed, so to ascribe feelings of guilt to an institution really amounts to ascribing it to particular persons within the institution. Institutions can have regret precisely because regrets don't entail responsibility, and where there is responsibility we look for particular agents. The president of Ivylawn, for example, could talk about the college having regrets without implying that she herself has them, but it would take a lot of work for her to say that the college feels guilty about something without giving the impression that she was talking about herself or other highly placed officials. It certainly is possible that there might be reports of such officials feeling "very badly" about what went on—not simply embarrassed, much more than regretful. Insofar as this means something like feeling "guilty," then if Taylor is right, such officials believe that while nothing is basically wrong with the institution, or with them, they or the institution bears responsibility for the racist events. The emphasis in action will be redeeming the good name of the institution and attending to the hurt done the injured parties as the means.

Let us go on to shame. Suppose the man who beats his wife feels shame for doing so. How is that different from his feeling em-

barrassed, or feeling guilty? According to Taylor (68), the identificatory belief in shame is that I am not the person I thought
I was or hoped I might be. It is not simply, as in embarrassment, that I wish I hadn't been seen doing something (even
though I don't think I've done anything wrong), or, as in guilt,
simply that I have failed to live up to a standard I adhere to.
If I thought the latter, I could still entertain the possibility
that I can set the record straight, for in such a case what
troubles me about what I've done is quite local: I've *done* something I don't approve of, but I'm not *someone* I don't approve
of. As Taylor puts it: "When feeling guilty . . . the view I take
of myself is entirely different from the view I take of myself
when feeling shame: in the latter case I see myself as being all
of a piece, what I have just done, I now see, fits only too well
what I really am. But when feeling guilty I think of myself as
having brought about a forbidden state of affairs and thereby
in this respect disfigured a self which otherwise remains the
same" (92).

So if Mr. Husband feels shame about beating his wife, he
must think that his action is revelatory of the person he in fact
is even though he had thought or hoped that he was someone
else, someone better than he turns out to be.

Thus Ivylawn College's possible feelings of shame about
the racism existing on its campus[21] would indicate that the
college, or people identified as its representatives, thought it
wasn't the institution it hoped it was. The racism on the campus is revelatory of what the institution really is, and not simply a sign that the college can't always live up to what it says it
stands for.

Perhaps that is why an institution is unlikely to feel or admit to shame: it may be unable to countenance the possibility that at root it is not what it purports, even to itself, to be.

FEMINISM, GUILT, AND SHAME

So, then, our emotions, or at least some of them, can be highly revelatory of who and what we care or don't care about. They provide powerful clues to the ways in which we take ourselves to be implicated in the lives of others and they in ours. And their absence provides such clues as much as their presence does.

What should we make of some white women's feelings of guilt in the face of charges by Black women, Latinas, Chinese American women, and others, that until very recently, so much of our theorizing has been heavily tilted in the direction and to the exclusive benefit of white middle-class Western women? Taylor's work suggests several reflections on the function of such guilt.

First, if Taylor is right about the point of action taken to get rid of the feeling of guilt, then guilt is not an emotion that makes us attend well to the situation of those whose treatment at our hands we feel guilty about. We're too anxious trying to keep our moral slate clean.

Secondly, I think it worth asking whether in any given case people are feeling guilt or rather simply embarrassment. If the latter, then there is no sense that one has failed to act in accordance with what one stands for. There are no amends to make, only appearances to create.

Third, I think that there is a neat fit between feeling guilty, and a particular way of conceiving the relation between one's gender and one's racial identity. This friendly cohabitation throws some interesting light on the concept of "white guilt." According to Taylor, in feeling guilt rather than shame, it is possible for me to think of a part of myself as not living up to what the rest of me stands for. Insofar as I see myself as "doer of a wicked deed" (134), I see the hint of an alien self; in order to make sure such a self does not emerge, I need to do whatever it takes to "purge" myself of this alien self (135). If I have a metaphysical position according to which my gender identity is thoroughly distinct from my racial identity (what I elsewhere call a form of "tootsie roll metaphysics"),[22] I can rely very handily on a neat distinction between myself as woman and myself as white person. The woman part of me is perfectly okay; it's being white that is the source of my wrongdoing. I assert my privilege over, say, a Latina, not insofar as I am a woman but insofar as I am white. Notice then that unless I am prepared to think of my womanness and my whiteness as folded inextricably into the person I am, I can think of myself and my responsibility for my acts in the following way: what really counts about me is that I am a woman, and my deeds do not show that I am not any less of a woman than I thought I was; it's only insofar as I am white, which isn't nearly as important a part of me, that I have failed other women. It's not the woman in me that failed the woman in you; it's the white in me that failed (for example) the Black in you. I, woman, feel nothing in particular; but I, white person, do feel guilt. If feminism focuses on the woman part of me, and the woman part of you, conceived of as thoroughly distinct from my white part and your Black part, feminism doesn't have to pay attention to our relations as white and Black. We never have to confront each other woman to woman, then, only white to Black, or Anglo to Latina.

The history of woman's inhumanity to woman is a shameful aspect of the history of women. However, I am not proposing a daily regimen of shame-inducing exercises. Nor do I think that the deep self-doubt that is part of shame can serve as the immediate ground of a vibrant feminist politics, a politics that expresses and promotes real care and concern for more than just a few women's lives. But I do not see how women who enjoy privileged status over other women (whether it be based on "race," class, religion, age, sexual orientation, physical mobility) can come to think it desirable to lose that privilege (by force or consent) unless they see it not only as producing harm to other women but also as being deeply disfiguring to themselves. It is not simply, as it would be in the case of guilt, that the point of ceasing to harm others is to remove a disquieting blot from one's picture of oneself. The deeper privilege goes, the less self-conscious people are of the extent to which their being who they are, in their own eyes as well as the eyes of others, is dependent upon the exploitation or degradation or disadvantage of others. Seeing oneself as deeply disfigured by privilege, and desiring to do something about it, may be impossible without feeling shame. The degree to which one is moved to undermine systems of privilege is closely tied to the degree to which one feels shame at the sort of person such privilege makes or allows one to be.

Lillian Smith's comment on her own upbringing as a young southern white girl in the early decades of the twentieth century reminds us that people who are taught that compassion is a virtue at the same time can be taught, perhaps usually are taught, that only some kinds of persons are the appropriate objects of their tender care. Whatever we mean by feminism, it ought not to make it difficult for us, following Smith's lead, to examine and evaluate how women treat or mistreat one another. Paradoxically, we run the risk of being diverted from such an examination by a focus on the contrast between an ethics of care and ethical systems that seem not to take care seriously. So far the contrast tells us nothing about who cares or does not care for whom. Moreover, since an ethics of care has been claimed to be associated strongly though not exclusively with the way women think and act in the moral domain, it makes it very hard even to suggest that some women have failed to care for others, let alone that they have done violence to others.

If thinking about the rhetoric of tragedy means thinking about over whom we grieve, and why, thinking about the rhetoric of care means thinking about for whom we care, and how.[23]

Chapter Five

CHANGING THE SUBJECT:
ON MAKING YOUR SUFFERING MINE

*O*ne of the striking features of the campaign waged by nineteenth-century white suffragists in the United States was their comparison of the plight of women to the plight of slaves. A not untypical formulation was expressed by Elizabeth Cady Stanton: "The prolonged slavery of women is the darkest page in human history."[1] The white women in question not only wanted to make sense of their situation to and for themselves; they also wanted it to be understood by others as a condition crying out for and requiring a remedy. While they knew full well that plenty of men—and women—might disagree with them or ignore them altogether, they were eager to have the rights of women considered "a legitimate branch of the anti-slavery enterprise."[2]

These considerations point to certain constraints on the

ways in which these suffragists would have to describe their suffering. First of all, it would have to be presented as something systemic, a general condition of women (not a peculiar condition of a few anomalous poor souls) for which a general remedy could be found. And their suffering would have to be given an appropriate value in what, to borrow a phrase from the historian Martin Pernick, we may call a societal "calculus of suffering."[3] That is, on the one hand, they certainly would want to preclude a depiction of their situation that would allow others to trivialize their plight, by comparing them to whining spoiled children, for example; on the other hand, they would have to be careful not to overstate the severity of their situation. And they certainly would want to avoid what we now might call the medicalization of their pain—a reading of their misery that suggested individualized mental or physical rehabilitation as the most appropriate remedy. In short, their suffering had to be presented in such a light that it would be seen as a moral, social, and legal issue, that is, an issue of social injustice; that it be seen as remediable; and that its severity be neither under- nor overstated. In such a context, it is not surprising that Stanton and other white women active in the movement to abolish slavery drew heavily upon the language and imagery of the experience of slavery to make sense of and bring attention to the social, legal, and economic contraints under which they lived.

In *Women and Sisters: The Antislavery Feminists in American Culture*, Jean Fagan Yellin has examined in considerable detail what she describes as the "application of antislavery discourse to the condition of women."[4] Yellin describes the means by which the subject of the experience of slavery was changed—

from Black male and female slave to white woman and, in a later development, to "humanity in general."

Yellin makes clear that the linking of the condition of Black female slaves and white middle-class women often was not tendered simply or cautiously as a limited analogy. Some of the most vigorous and committed of white female abolitionists came to regard themselves as slaves, to describe their own experience in terms appropriated whole cloth from the language developed to depict slavery: as such women "expanded their discussions of the condition of slaves to include discussions of the condition of women, they continued to use the same discursive codes, but they connected them to new referends."[5] White women spoke not simply of being slaves, as in the quotation above from Stanton, but talked of being bound, fettered, having the oppressor's foot on their necks.[6] Yellin cites a passage from the diary of Angelina Grimké in which Grimké begins with a clear reference to a slave, but then proceeds, as Yellin puts it, to focus "on herself, describing her own transformation into a powerless slave. The passivity, the apprehension—the shaking knees, the sinking heart, the prayer for strength—all are her own. The suffering painfully recounted is Grimké's own. As she writes, the black woman recedes."[7] In the hands of Grimké and others, the subject changes not only from female slave to a particular white woman, but then to women in general, though that in practice meant white woman in general, or rather white middle-class Christian woman in general.[8] In either case, the female slave is made to disappear from view. Although presumably it was the female slave's experience that originally was the focus of concern, other women's experiences were made the focus.

Thus, although Yellin in no way underestimates the considerable hardship and violence to which white, nonslave women were subject, her work invites us to consider to what degree such women appropriated the experience of Black slaves, and Black female slaves in particular, that is, the extent to which they presented themselves as occupying the same experiential territory as slaves while erasing signs of the slaves' occupation of that territory. Yellin's concerns here are not unlike those expressed by the contemporary Black feminist bell hooks, who, in the opening pages of her *feminist theory: from margin to center*, insists that "feminist emphasis on 'common oppression' in the United States was less a strategy for politicization than an appropriation by conservative and liberal women of a radical political vocabulary that masked the extent to which they shaped the movement so that it addressed and promoted their class interests."[9]

Many of us no doubt share these concerns. But, as Yellin's work illustrates, there is a host of important issues that remain unexamined if all we say here is that white women illegitimately appropriated the experience of Black women. Yellin's book gives us the chance to take a close look at some of the early moments in the long history of the tension between white and Black women active in abolitionist, civil rights, and women's struggles in the nineteenth and twentieth centuries in the United States as they tried to make sense of their own and one another's suffering. Along the way, too, Yellin encourages us to look at some perplexing issues that arise when we think about the complex social and political conditions in which claims about the shared subjectivity of experiences typically are made. For as Yellin's work makes clear, some white suffragists' use of the language of slavery to describe the situation of women had a complicated and contradictory relation to the institutionalized white racism of the time: in some ways it undermined, in some ways it sustained such racism. This paradoxical relation took at least three closely related forms, which I call the paradox in appropriation, the paradox in identification, and the paradox in universality.

THE PARADOX IN APPROPRIATION

What I am calling "paradoxes" represent ways in which white women's comparison of themselves to slaves could both subvert and sustain the institutions of white supremacy in the context of which the comparisons were made. The first of these paradoxes, the paradox in appropriation, serves as a reminder that while the self-interested appropriation by white women of the experience of Black women was and is noxious, so surely would be a failure or refusal by white women to find or make anything in common with Black women.

For example, Linda Brent, the voice of the ex-slave Harriet A. Jacobs in *Incidents in the Life of a Slave Girl, Written by Herself*,[10] hoped that the northern white women she addressed would understand the significance of their shared experience as mothers, even while she expressed keen awareness that there was much about slavery the white women could not understand.

June Jordan recently expressed her astonishment at a well-meaning white woman's resolute inability or unwillingness to see or imagine that she and Jordan have any shared experiences or concerns. Jordan describes the white woman sitting across from her in her office, "friendly as an old stuffed animal, beaming good will" toward her as she recites with bizarre envy the important problems Jordan, as an African American, has to face: "poverty, violence, discrimination in general."[11] Such envious glorification of Jordan's experience turns Jordan into an exotic and alien sufferer. In this connection it is instructive to remember María Lugones's reference to the "complex failure of love in the failure to identify with another woman, the failure to see oneself in other women who are quite different from oneself."[12]

Perhaps now the paradox is becoming clear: while there certainly seems to be something repugnant in seeing so much of oneself in another's experience that one completely obscures the existence of that other subject, there is something similarly repugnant in so distancing oneself from the experiences of others that one cannot see oneself as having anything to do with such an experience or with anyone who has had such an experience.[13]

Similarly, the idea that one can put on another's experiences, the way in which you might slip on her coat, is an almost incoherent notion that can take grotesque expressions, as in designer "homelessness" fashions displayed on storefront manikins draped in sleeping bags: make a fashion statement by putting on the experience of homelessness; or, perhaps, as an ad in the *New York Times* suggests: men, wear Calvin Klein blue jeans, and make people think you've had the experience of being one of the workers who dug the subway tunnels of Manhattan. There are experiences we desperately don't want to have had, but we seem ready to attach ourselves, at a safe distance, to any glamour that is associated with such experiences. To borrow a phrase my mother used in another context, some of us use others as "spiritual bellhops," relieved that they actually have had experiences we simply want to have the appearance of having had.[14]

And yet, despite the ever-present possibility of such exploitative sentimentality—and here again is the tension, the paradox, in appropriation—it would be absurd to deny that in some important sense people can and should try to put on the experiences of others.

To return to the historical moment about which Yellin is writing, the hope of slaves that others might understand the trouble they had seen, and be moved to do something about it, seems to be linked in some way with the possibility that others could be the subjects of such suffering even though in fact they were not.[15] Slaves, and the abolitionists who hoped to relieve their plight, certainly counted on the possibility that those who were not slaves could both understand claims about the horrors of slavery and be moved to act out of the belief that the experiences undergone by slaves were the kind that *no* subject should have. That is, slaves and abolitionists presumably thought that others could know enough about what it is, or what it would be, to be the subject of such experiences, that they would act to prevent those experiences being those of *anyone*.

And so it would be odd to hope that nonslaves would understand and have compassion for slaves and yet at the same time not allow that nonslaves might themselves be or become the subjects of such suffering or something very much like it. As Lawrence Blum has argued, compassion involves simultaneously both a difference in the actual situation of the sufferer and the compassionate person *and* a sense of their shared vulnerability to suffering. In compassion, I am moved by what *you* are going through, not what *I* am going through, concerned about *your* condition, not about *mine*.[16] At the same time, while I need not have gone through what you have, your "suffering . . . is seen as the kind of thing that could happen to anyone, including [my]self insofar as [I] am a human being."[17] My sense that I too could be a subject of such suffering, far from occluding or erasing your status as the subject of suffering about whom I am concerned, expresses my belief in our shared humanity. I see you not only as a subject of suffering but your susceptibility to it as something we share. In fact, following Blum, we can say that my acknowledgment of the possibility that the subject of suffering can change distinguishes the person who has compassion from the one who merely pities: in pity, Blum says, "one holds oneself apart from the afflicted person and from their suffering, thinking of it as something that defines the person as fundamentally different from oneself."[18] While I in principle could be the subject of the kind of experience you are having, insofar as I pity you, I wouldn't be caught dead, in fact, having such an experience, presumably because of a belief I have that goes like this: certain kinds of experiences are had only by certain kinds of people, and by gum, I'm not *that* kind of person, or at least not insofar as and in the respects in which such a person is pitiful. We will return to this interesting alleged connection between kinds of experiences and kinds of persons.[19]

In sum, the paradox in appropriation reminds us that seeing one's own experience in the experience of others can all too easily lend itself to the expropriation of the experiences of others, to putting their experiences to one's own use while erasing the fact of their having been subjects of those experiences. But at the same time, our thinking of one another as possible subjects of the same kinds of experiences can be an important piece of our thinking of one another as members of the same human community.

But if our thinking of one another as possible subjects of the same kinds of experiences is part of our thinking of one another as members of the same human community, it ought not to be surprising to find that individuals or groups who wish to distinguish themselves from other individuals or groups try to do so by insisting that they would never be subjects of the kinds of experiences the others have, and the others could never be subjects of the kinds of experiences they have. Philosophers need turn no further than Plato and Aristotle for telling examples.

Many of the paeans to Love produced by the near-tipsy revelers in Plato's *Symposium* insist that the capacity for experiencing real Love is not distributed equally among human subjects. The idea that real Love involves a kind of experience only intelligent and educated subjects can have, alluded to first in Pausanias' distinction between Common and Heavenly Love, is given more explicit articulation in Socrates' account of the lessons he learned from Diotima. There is an experience that the lover can have only after much preparation, and Diotima's description of this culminating experience is really quite glorious: "You see [she says to Socrates], the man who has been thus far educated in matters of Love, who has beheld beautiful things in the right order and correctly, is coming now to the goal of Loving: all of a sudden he will catch sight of something wonderfully beautiful in its nature; that, Socrates, is the reason for all his earlier labors" (210e–211a). This experience is that of "see[ing] the Beautiful itself, absolute, pure, unmixed, not polluted by human flesh or colors or any other great nonsense of mortality" (211e).[20] This kind of promise isn't anything like what one of the major television networks offered up in an advertisement a few years ago for its broadcast of the upcoming World Series: "the memories are waiting." The experience of the Beautiful that the thoroughly prepared Socratic lover will have is not something just anyone can have, not something democratically awaiting any and all who happen to turn their eyes and ears a given direction at a given time. Love is a laborious enterprise, not an experience either a couch potato or a person otherwise making use of a couch can be guaranteed to have.

But Diotima's point is not simply that some experiences can only be had after long and difficult preparation. Some people just *cannot* experience the Beautiful itself. While the lover, in "unstinting love of wisdom," that is, in *philosophia* (210d), finally catches sight of Beauty itself, a servant thinks beauty can be beheld in "a single example." Like the "boys and women" referred to in the *Republic* (557c) "when they see bright-colored things," the servant will "favor the beauty of a little boy or a man or a single custom" (210d). Diotima explains: "being a slave, of course, he's low and small-minded" (210d) and doesn't know, can't know, the distinction between a beautiful thing and Beauty itself.

It is no secret that Plato thought there were different kinds of humans and that though an ideal human community is made up of many kinds—philosopher-rulers, guardians, artisans, and (Socrates barely notes it) slaves—the type of person you are is determined by your mental capacity, including the capacity for certain levels of education. Those whose natural capacities and careful education mark them out as real lovers of wisdom will have experiences that just will not be available to others.

This doesn't mean Plato thought there were *no* experiences of which both philosophers and others could be subjects. Nor did Aristotle, though in his work, as in Plato's, distinctions among humans are mirrored in distinctions among their possible experiences (a "natural slave" of Aristotle's surely is not a possible subject of tragic experience as understood by Aristotle[21]). A danger always lurking for both Plato and Aristotle is the possibility that rationally well endowed individuals will have experiences of a kind that will erode or distort or leave underdeveloped their rationality. As Terence Irwin has reminded us, Aristotle "prohibits the citizens of his ideal state from menial work, because such work is inconsistent with the virtue that is required for a happy life ([*Politics*] 1328b–1329a). In [Aristotle's] view, someone who must spend most of his time and effort working for a precarious living, or in dependence on the favor of another, will never develop the right virtues of character for a citizen."[22] Aristotle insists that "no man can practice excellence who is living the life of a mechanic or laborer" (*Politics* 1278a20; cf. 1319a27)—leisure is necessary for that (*Politics* 1329a11).[23] So even though well-educated citizens could in principle have some of the same experiences as free laborers and artisans, or as slaves, they could do so only on pain of eroding crucial differences between themselves and those more "lowly" types. "Certainly the good man and the statesman and the good citizen ought not to learn the crafts of inferiors except for their own occasional use; if they habitually practice them, there will cease to be a distinction between master and slave" (*Politics* 1277b4–7).

Our inquiry into the possibility of one person or group appropriating the experience of another individual or group has led us to some reflections on both the ontological status of experience as something that can have more than one subject, and the moral significance of different human beings thinking of each other as possible subjects of the same kinds of experience. We have just seen recognition of these features of experience in the insistence on the part of philosophers such as Plato and Aristotle—for whom metaphysical differences in kinds of human subjects justify claims for maintaining political distinctions among them—that some humans have important kinds of experiences that other humans just can't have, and that while there are some kinds of experiences any human can have, some humans should not have them. Slaves just can't have the experiences only true lovers of wisdom can; while good citizens can have the experiences menial laborers have, they should not, on pain of eroding the distinction between these types of human beings. (An advertisement in *The New Yorker* reminds us of yet another way in which claims to exclusive access to certain kinds of experiences are meant to distinguish some kinds of people from others: there are, the resort ad tells us, "pleasures few will know," since "our number of guests are limited."[24])

Having seen the investment in the idea that there are sorts of experiences only certain kinds of people can have, and experiences only certain kinds of people should have, let us return to the world in which the Black and white women about whom Yellin writes lived and thought and did political battle. In particular, let us return to the ways in which white women's attempted identification with Black female slaves had a paradoxical relation to the white supremacy of the time, both subverting it, by conflating the experiences of whites and Blacks, and yet also expressing it, by obscuring the white women's own role in the maintenance of slavery.

THE PARADOX IN IDENTIFICATION

The comparison of the situation of women and slaves, which of course doesn't make sense at all as a comparison unless the women in question were *not* slaves, occurred in a context in which whites' alleged superiority over Blacks was being affirmed in and through every major institution of the society. Even white abolitionists, male and female, did not necessarily seek to undermine white supremacy. For ending slavery was fully compatible with maintaining segregation and systematic inequality between whites and Blacks, with outlawing mixed-race marriages and imposing heavy sanctions on mixed-race alliances. The use of the image of slavery to describe the situation of white women involved a powerful trope intended to point to deep, significant, and compelling similarities in the experiences of two groups of people whose differences it was the main busi-

ness of the dominant racial ideology otherwise to insist upon.
Thus there is good reason to believe that in the eyes of those
wishing to maintain white supremacy, the conceptual miscege-
nation (the concept is borrowed from Toni Morrison[25]) conflating the experience of white women with that of Black female
slaves could have been seen as almost as damaging to the alleged
purity of white experience and its crucial distinctiveness from
Black experience as the sexual union of whites and Blacks would
be to the alleged purity and distinctiveness of white blood. As
Yellin reminds us,[26] taking seriously the identity of the situation
of white and Black women would mean that there were no significant differences between them—at least for the purposes of
the antislavery campaign. Now, as mentioned earlier, such a
claim would seem to undermine pervasive racist ideology,
which can't allow for any occasions in which skin color doesn't
make a difference. It is difficult for dominating groups to maintain their sense of superiority without both having and believing an ideology according to which those allegedly inferior
to and in fact subordinate to them are not as fully human as
they themselves are. And, as we saw in our brief foray into the
work of Plato and Aristotle, such an ideology is well-nigh impossible if the more powerful group seriously entertains the
idea that the experiences of the subordinates are a rich human
resource, rich enough in any event to serve the superior interests and describe the superior lives of the dominant group. The
more intent a dominating group is on maintaining its difference from and superiority to a subordinate group, surely the
less likely it is to allow that the experiences of the subordinate
group are adequate to describe the dominant group, let alone in
any way preferable to its own such resources.

But on the other hand—and hence the paradox in identification—such assertions of identity also served to reinforce racism, to the degree that the claim of identity obscured the real difference that race made to the situations of the two groups of women. In particular, it obscured the role of white women themselves in maintaining the institutions of white supremacy, in helping, through their everyday interactions with Black slaves, to add to the suffering. For the representation of one as a cosufferer obscures whatever role one plays as a perpetrator of the misery.

THE PARADOX IN UNIVERSALITY

Finally, let us turn to the third version of the paradox, which goes something like this: in the context of institutionalized racism, claims about the "universality" of a dominated group's experience can be used both to subvert and to sustain those institutions.

At least one reason for a group's calling upon the experiences of other people, even those the group considers their cultural inferiors, is to try to make sense of one's own painful situation: maybe somebody *has* known the trouble I've seen. And, as Toni Morrison has said in a related context, "comparisons are a major form of knowledge and flattery."[27] The very facts that allowed us to see the white female abolitionists' comparison between themselves and female slaves as a brazen affront to white supremacist ideology also invite us to see the comparison as a kind of flattery—the kind of flattery no doubt intended by the editors of the *Boston Globe* when they described the photography exhibit "I Dream a World: Portraits of Black Women Who Changed America" as "speak[ing] to the potential inside everyone";[28] the flattery no doubt intended by a biographer of the artist Frida Kahlo when the writer said in the pages of the *New York Times* that when Kahlo "displays her wounds we immediately know that those wounds stand for all human suffering";[29] the flattery no doubt intended by those who insist that descriptions of the experiences of a historically marginalized group don't just capture their particular lives but in fact tell us something significant about the lives of all people. In this connection, Mary Helen Washington has noted the trivializing effect of the treatment of Black women's writing as "singular and anomalous, not universal and representative."[30] It may then seem churlish to subject the white female abolitionists' comparison between themselves and female slaves to the kind of scrutiny it has gotten in Yellin's book and in my comments. The white women were, after all, trying desperately to make sense of and give voice to what was without doubt a difficult existence, and by comparing themselves to female slaves they were also suggesting that the lives of the slaves had significance beyond the slaves themselves.

However, an analysis like Yellin's demonstrates that the comparison tended neither to promote anyone's knowledge nor to honor anyone's experience. First of all, the comparison for the most part was not the fruit of discussions among white and Black women about their relative situations and the meaning or meanings of their suffering. Collaboration of sorts was not entirely out of the question: Harriet Jacobs was helped by Amy Post and Lydia Maria Child, both white abolitionists; Harriet

Beecher Stowe offered to include an account of Jacobs's life in *The Key to Uncle Tom's Cabin*, though Jacobs demurred because she wanted to write her own story.[31] But for obvious reasons discussions among Black and white women were not likely to take place, or to involve much mutual comprehension even if they did. In the absence of exchanges between the two groups of women, there was no way for white women to test their interpretations of the meaning of slavery for Black women, especially when white women portrayed Black women as reduced, either by nature or by circumstance, to virtual speechlessness about the matter.[32]

Second, if the white women's situation really was the same as that of Black women, the white women could just as well speak about it as the Black women. If the experience of Black women is treated as the experience of everybody, this can easily diminish rather than enlarge the significance of it: how can they have anything special or particular to say, if their experience is really no different from universal human experience? One can't here but think of the anger and worry expressed by those historians of the Holocaust—many of whom are from families who directly suffered under it—who are alarmed by what one has called "the glib equation of the murder of the Jews with any disaster or atrocity, with any state of affairs one abhors or even merely dislikes."[33] The point Lucy Dawidowicz wishes to make here is not that no suffering matches that of the Holocaust; rather, she says, the facile equation of the destruction of the European Jews with any and all other atrocities "obscur[es] the role of anti-Semitism in accomplishing that murder."[34]

To the extent that white women saw themselves as identifying with Black women they perhaps were in effect asserting what Karl Morrison describes as the central proposition of empathy: "I Am You."[35] Morrison makes some telling points about the nature of the relationship that is affirmed thereby. The empathetic participation "in the affliction of another, making it [one's] own,"[36] is compatible with, indeed may itself enact, an imposition of the person feeling the empathy on the person for whom the empathy is felt. As Morrison reads the history of the claim, there were two powerful paradigms for understanding how an "I" can become a "You": a biological one, which involved male dominance over female; and an aesthetic one, involving "the imposition of form by the artist on recalcitrant matter."[37]

This characteristic of empathy is related to what Morrison calls the "non-dialogic" aspect of it—when empathy is "one-sided" rather than "interpersonal," when one person participates in the experiences of another but not vice versa, when the identity affirmed is so complete as to negate the possibility of a distinction between two different people.[38] There is always the danger that the person claiming to participate in the experience of another is simply a ventriloquist.[39]

In sum, if Morrison is right, empathy does not necessarily reflect or encourage knowledge; having it does not require recognizing another as separate, nor hearing what they may have to say about the empathetic gesture or about what is claimed to be understood. Inequality along most any dimension is not at all ruled out by empathy; indeed, if Morrison is right, the paradigms out of which the understanding of "I Am You" was shaped historically are ones of domination and imposition.[40]

The point here is not to mount a campaign against empathy but simply to note some of its features. Empathy of this sort does not require trying to elicit from the afflicted their view about their pain. Early in her book Yellin points out ways in which white female abolitionists seemed to assume that the meaning of the slave's suffering was obvious. But at the same time, anyone presented as in need of empathy in this way is presented as in need of a ventriloquist, should any questions arise about her state or what ought to be done about it. To say this is not to condemn empathy but only to point out why it differs from what one party feels toward the other when both are actually in the same situation, when each is in a position to offer her own interpretation of her situation and to act in her own behalf.

The work of Jean Fagan Yellin and others has led us to think about the idea of one group's appropriation of the experience of another group. What is involved in such appropriation, and under what conditions is it troubling?

I have sketched out three paradoxes to footnote Yellin's sense of the complexity of answers to such questions. The paradox in appropriation suggests that while a danger in assuming the experiences of others is that they as subjects of such experiences will be erased, a danger in *refusing* to do so is that one may thereby deny the possibility of a shared humanity. The paradox in identification reminds us that while the formula "women are slaves" tended to subvert white supremacy by denying differences between Black and white women, the formula sustained white supremacy insofar as it obscured white women's roles in supporting slavery. And the paradox in universality cautions that while calling on the experience of a marginalized group to represent "human experience" can be an important way of honoring that group's experience, it also can be a way of trivializing and thus further marginalizing them.

In short, there seems to be nothing inherently disturbing in a person's thinking of herself or himself as the subject of the same kind of experience that another person has had. Indeed, the possibility of shared experience seems in some circumstances to be part of an expression of shared humanity.

But humans are ingenious in devising ways to deny such shared status even when appearing to affirm it. Whites in the United States have made Blacks undergo experiences meant to mark them as different from whites, and one of the most powerful of these was slavery. Despite the severe difficulties of their own lives, for the white women Yellin discusses to have used the language of slavery to depict their own condition was to try to reap something useful for themselves from the experience of slavery without having endured its horrors in the ways that slaves did. It no doubt was a measure of their desperation that they presented themselves as subjects of such suffering. But it was also a measure of their relative power that they could so readily put on the mantle of slavery to make sense of their own condition.[41]

Chapter Six

ON THE AESTHETIC
USABILITY OF SUFFERING

*W*e *have just looked at some* worries that arise when, in order to bring attention to their own plight, individuals or groups appear to recycle the suffering of others exploitatively. But of course struggles for political recognition or economic justice don't provide the only examples of concerns about the use and abuse of suffering. A related series of questions surfaces in response to artistic representations of human misery and pain: under what conditions does such art scavenge the suffering of those portrayed? Under what conditions, on the other hand, does it serve those suffering? Or does raising such questions betray a misunderstanding of the meaning and function of art? Is art, properly understood, a domain so separate from social and political struggle that we need not worry whether the representation of suffering ever becomes, for example, simply a vehicle for the aesthetic experience of the viewer or the enhanced reputation of the artist?

These and related inquiries about the relation between art and suffering have long been the staple of a certain strand of art criticism. They arose in a particularly pointed way in the wake of an instantly notorious *New Yorker* piece by the eminent American dance critic, Arlene Croce.[1] Croce announced her refusal to attend and review Bill T. Jones's *Still/Here* on the grounds that the piece violated the aesthetic conditions under which human suffering—in this case, AIDS and other terminal illnesses—can become the proper stuff of art in general and of dance theater in particular.

Croce's essay reminds us that art today no less than in the time of Plato is among the more visible and commanding means by which attention is brought to suffering. But art cannot do this without being implicated in a host of moral and political struggles over whose suffering is attended to, how it is attended to, and who benefits from the ways such suffering is focused and framed. As we shall see, Croce appears to want to cabin off art from morality and politics. But her attempt to do so paradoxically shows the impossibility of achieving that when suffering is the subject of art.

CROCE'S LAMENT: A PRELIMINARY SKETCH

There are multiple layers of concern in Croce's short article. At the core is her certainty that the HIV-positive Jones, armed with videotapes of people suffering from AIDS and other serious ill-nesses, has "taken sanctuary among the unwell" (60) and that *Still/Here* consists predominantly of the parading of people "who are terminally ill and talk about it" (54). Under such cir-cumstances, she insists, there is no possible role for the critic. The critic's "primary task" is to evaluate the performance (58), but the only possible response to the presence of dying people is to feel sorry for them (55).[2]

Clearly, though, Croce believes the critic has some other tasks in addition to evaluating performances, or her piece would lack justification altogether. So of what else ought the critic to speak, if the primary reason for speaking has been de-nied her? Having told us that she cannot even begin to say whether *Still/Here* is good dance or bad dance because such a vocabulary is inappropriate in reaction to the presentation of actual suffering and death, she perforce invokes and patrols the distinction between art and nonart, between dance and non-dance. Croce makes clear that given what she takes to be "the express intentions" of *Still/Here*, there is no reason to regard it as dance theater (54). This is not performance, not art, not dance, but rather a "messianic travelling medicine show, de-signed to do some good for sufferers of fatal illnesses, both those in the cast and those thousands more who may be in the audi-ence" (54). A dance critic as such responds only to dance. This is not dance. So Arlene Croce, as dance critic, cannot respond to it.

Is she implying, then, that anything that has to do with suffering can't be the subject of art? That would be an absurd position and it clearly is not that of Croce, who explicitly sets out to compare what she takes to be Jones's treatment of suffering and death with what she regards as the aesthetically and spiritually rewarding treatments by the likes of Keats, Chopin, Schumann, and the contemporary playwrights David and Ain Gordon. So it is the way that suffering is taken up in *Still/Here* (which she claims to know about even though she did not see it) that makes the piece "unintelligible as theatre" (54). According to Croce, the Romantics dealt successfully with death by "transcending" it, by which she seems to mean some combination of the following: not mentioning one's own situation (59); allowing the artistic impulse to outshine and dwarf the illness, thereby prohibiting one's situation from being reduced to a pathological condition (59); refusing to have one's individual identity dissolved into an identity as a member of an oppressed or diseased group (59–60).

In the absence of such transcendence, there is no art, only unmediated or barely mediated suffering and death. There are no actors or dancers, only sufferers. Whatever audiences get out of observing such suffering, it cannot be the experience of art and its accompanying transcendence. There is the positive danger that in such circumstances audiences are reduced to voyeurs (54) or mere patrons of pain (55); in any event, like the professional critic, audiences are denied the opportunity of doing the hard work of evaluating the performance (60).

Croce's despair about the absence of art, the irrelevance of the critic, and the dumbing down of the audience appears in the context of her critique of what she sees as the cultural convergence of the celebration of victimhood and funding agencies' predilection for "socially useful" art (56): scarce resources go to the historically silenced, downtrodden, abused, in hopes of improving not only their situation but that of the audiences, who can learn through the power of art to be sympathetic to the plight of those less fortunate.

Croce says she is fed up with finding herself so "manipulated," "intimidated," and "cowed" by the suffering humanity presented in performances such as *Still/Here* that she is denied an appropriate roost from which to provide critical appraisal. But this does not deflect or disable her from carrying out what she implies are other tasks of the dance critic: providing general guidelines for distinguishing between art and nonart; worrying about the aesthetic, moral, and political costs of failing to understand that distinction; and commenting on the conditions under which suffering can properly be taken up by art. Indeed, with respect to all these matters we can extract a kind of credo from Croce's *New Yorker* article.

The Crocean Credo[3]

(#1) Dance does not exist in order to make dancers or audiences feel good or feel bad or feel compassionate or feel guilty. If there actually is dance going on—as opposed, for example, to a "messianic travelling medicine show"—the artists must be presenting what they are doing as dance, not as therapy of any kind. The intention of the artists in this regard must be clear to the audience (54).

The audience in its turn has to be prepared to understand and look for the expression of such intention:

(#2) If you are going to the dance, you have to be going for the dancing, not for healing, not for a political rally (54).

Indeed, failing to understand the distinction between dance performance and whatever else might be going on in the theater may well expose audiences to pernicious moral dangers. Those attending performances such as *Still/Here* should be forewarned:

(#3) Audiences should not expect or allow themselves to be voyeurs of others' suffering (54).

But this is all too likely to happen in a piece like *Still/Here*, for

(#4) Performers fail their audiences aesthetically and morally when they parade actual suffering before the audience. They fail them aesthetically, because the mere parading of suffering, however moving, is not performance. They fail them morally, because audiences are being put in a position where either they are simply voyeurs of the suffering of others (54); or, if forced to feel sorry for sufferers (55), deprived of the free exercise of their moral agency; or they are provided the temptation to patronize the sufferers through applause (55).

What compromises the audience aesthetically and morally thoroughly disables the critic:

(#5) As long as the mere presentation of suffering is what is on stage, there is no role for the critic to play (55). Critics develop

and deploy standards of evaluation (56). One cannot evaluate the suffering of others. One can only feel compassion (55).

But even then, as implied in (#4), compassion of one person for another may easily be confused with a meretricious relationship:

(#6) Compassion should not be confused with complicity in the following arrangement: you put sufferers on stage, I'll feel sorry for them, and we'll all call it art (55).

This takes us back to Croce's concerns about the proper role of art:

(#7) The view that art can be constituted by such complicitous contracts, as in (#6), is a species of the view that art can and should be socially useful (56)—that it can and should advance what are considered morally and politically praiseworthy attitudes and behavior. Art is disinterested (56). That is, it is not necessarily socially useful, and even when it is, that is not what makes it art, let alone good art. What is socially useful can be bad art or no art at all.

According to Croce, the distinction between art and that which is socially useful has important implications for the role of the critic:

(#8) Standards about the goodness or badness of the dance are distinct from standards by which its social usefulness or worth-

> lessness is to be judged. *Dance critics cannot and should not be*
> *in the business of assessing a work's social usefulness. If that is*
> *all there is to assess, there is no art, and no role for the critic.*

Croce does not rule out the possibility that art, and presumably, more specifically, dance, can be about suffering. However, she insists that

> *(#9) While it is fine for art to depict suffering, the mere presen-*
> *tation of suffering cannot constitute art.*

This leaves us with the crucial question of just how, according to Croce, we are to distinguish between the mere parading of suffering and the artistic rendering of it. Her comments on transcendence sketch out an answer:

> *(#10) Art can be about suffering as long as the art rescues or*
> *transcends the suffering—for example, by exhibiting that one*
> *is not reduced to one's suffering, that one's "individual spirit"*
> *is more powerful and more important than one's disease or*
> *death (59). At the same time, getting beyond the suffering of a*
> *single individual simply by noting her membership in a larger*
> *group of sufferers doesn't constitute "transcendence." The pro-*
> *duction of art is to be distinguished from the certification of*
> *one's victim status (60).*

Arlene Croce, dance critic, turns out to be a choreographer as well—not of dancers and their movements, but of the experience of the dance. The appropriate performance and experience of the dance depends upon all the participants—performers, audience, critics—clearly understanding the complex constraints under which they are to operate. These constraints have to do with the intentions performers are allowed to realize in dance; the legitimate expectations audiences may bring to the dance; and the modes of human expressiveness appropriate as subjects for critics to comment upon.

THE AESTHETIC AND THE MORAL

Such constraints are as much moral as they are aesthetic; indeed, the aesthetic is mainly inseparable from the moral in Croce's essay. To say this may seem to be at odds with Croce's clear allegiance to the view that the production of art is to be distinguished from the doing of moral or political good, let alone the doing of moral or political evil (compare #7 and #8). But that allegiance itself is hardly morally or politically neutral. More specifically, the line she draws between art and nonart is in many respects a moral one, that is, it is cast in moral terminology. First of all, dancers shouldn't be—on her account cannot be, or what they do cannot count as dance—in the business of inviting audiences to ogle people suffering from terminal illnesses or diseases. Dancers shouldn't provide audiences with occasions for congratulating themselves for applauding those willing to expose their suffering publicly. Dancers shouldn't deprive audiences of authentic reactions to the suffering of others by manipulating them into feeling a particular way.

And for their part, audiences shouldn't allow themselves to be manipulated in any of these ways. Why not? Not only because they are confusing art with medicine shows or political rallies, but also and inseparably because these particular forms of confusion are morally compromising: it is indecent to be dazzled by the suffering of others, even worse to think of oneself as being a good person for doing so. Morally vigilant people should be on the lookout for occasions when their moral agency is undermined by deals according to which their willingness to have compassion forced out of them is sanctified by calling it an aesthetic response. Croce seems to assume that in general we don't like to be emotionally manipulated—or shouldn't like to be emotionally manipulated—but that we may fail to be on guard against that if we think, however wrongly, however hopefully, that we are in the presence of art.

The constraints that Croce sees imposed on the critic also are laced with moral concerns. If critics are confronted with unmediated, or barely mediated, human suffering, it would be inappropriate, indeed indecent, to comment on the sufferers' performance. In fact, Croce insists, it would be impossible to comment on their performance, because there is no performance, there is just their suffering. It would be bizarre at the very least, and surely just plain cruel, to comment on how well or how poorly they are suffering, to judge how one person's suffering stacks up against another's. The critic ought to be prepared to evaluate the success of artistic renderings of suffering, but not to appraise unmediated or barely mediated suffering itself. Art is different from life; art critics scrutinize performances, not lives.

Again, saying that the constraints Croce imposes on critics are inseparable from moral constraints is only apparently at odds with her insistence that art and art criticism are distinct from moral and political concerns. She is assuming that there are some things that critics as morally responsible persons should not do—for example, judge the suffering of others— just as there are some things that performers and audiences as morally sensitive persons should not do—derive cheap thrills from parading suffering or watching such a parade. Whatever is going on cannot be art if it requires such moral compromise from performers, audiences, and critics.

So far I have been taking Croce at her word about why she refused to attend *Still/Here.* In terms of dance, or performance, or art, there is, she insists, no *there* there, simply barely mediated suffering, and the only decent response to such suffering is compassion, not critical evaluation.

But perhaps I have taken her at only half her word. For her comments suggest not that her only possible response could be compassion, but rather—contra #5—that her actual response is contempt: in an oft-repeated phrase from her essay, she refers to how she is "*forced* to feel sorry for . . . dissed blacks, abused women, or disfranchised homosexuals" (55; emphasis in original). As we have seen, such comments can be taken as a warning about the variety of moral perils to which audiences (including critics) are subject, having, for example, something as important as concern for the suffering of others forced out of one. At the same time, it is hard not to hear the sneer in "dissed blacks, abused women, or disfranchised homosexuals"—a barely disguised snarl to the effect that the suffering portrayed doesn't deserve our attention. This isn't real suffering; this is the hyperbolic pain of professional victims.

To the extent to which this is Croce's response, her position is less that the suffering on stage is so unmediated as to compel our compassion and nothing else than that what is being staged is clumsily mediated suffering parading as art. This is the studied expression of suffering, so bloated by artistic pretense and political overkill as not to be worthy of our attention as art or as the kind of real suffering that deserves our compassionate response.

And if this is indeed what Croce is up to, then her position in "Discussing the Undiscussable" is not that *Still/Here* doesn't provide the right conditions for the discussion of suffering, but that the suffering in question is not worth representing or discussing. The likelihood that the latter is in fact her position is strengthened by the appearance of other reviews of *Still/Here* in which critics had no trouble raising questions about the dance's treatment of the suffering to which it brings our attention.

Not everyone who saw the piece felt forced into feeling sorry for the sufferers or was diverted, by what Croce assumed was barely mediated suffering, into having their critical faculties put on hold. For example, the dance critic Lynn Garafola, writing in the *Nation*, insisted that what is troubling about *Still/Here* is "not that it puts its 'victims' onstage but that it trivializes and betrays them."[4] And it does this, according to Garafola, not only through what she calls its "cavalier" use of the videotapes of ill people, but in and through the choreography and the dancing. "Jones has little sense of structure and little feeling for the physical logic of a phrase"; in "the second, chaotic half of the work . . . blinking images, a deafening score and aggressive, nonstop movement not only dwarf the human drama but also preclude any expression of empathy" (37). So to a dance critic who actually saw *Still/Here*, the problem is not that one is railroaded into feeling sorry for ill people, but rather that the proper attention to the subject at hand is made impossible by poor choreography and uninspired performance.

In light of criticisms like Garafola's, the praise Croce received in some quarters for her attack on "victim art"[5] seems misplaced. Despite her lament that "I do not remember a time when the critic has seemed more expendable than now" (Croce, 60)—echoed in Deborah Jowitt's sympathetic "she's not alone in feeling her critical prerogatives and her power hobbled by art that prompts pity for the artists because of social oppression or the precarious state of their health"[6]—Croce seems to have thrown off the critic's mantle, not had it ripped from her. The fierce critic of "victim art" has, not to put too fine a point on it, claimed victim status for herself. She has taken the easy way out: she has complained about being unable to judge this particular piece on its artistic merits, insisting that the grounds for making such a judgment—up or down—have been pulled out from under her.

ART AND SUFFERING: QUESTIONS ABOUT THE CROCEAN CREDO

Many readers no doubt will remain puzzled about Croce's actual motivation, and about her refusal to do straightforwardly what at least some other critics were quite willing to do: to try to explain why they thought the actual performance of *Still/Here* failed, and failed *artistically*, to deal appropriately with the experiences of human suffering it presents to the audience. Nonetheless, whatever her actual motivation, we have from Croce a vehement statement of the view that art should keep us at the right distance from suffering. On such a view, sufferers suffering is not art because it puts the audience much too close to the suffering, offering too thin a mediation between audience and raw human experience. One important clue to the absence of the appropriate distance is that the performance makes us feel sorry for the performers' condition, rather than interested in the performance itself. A performance's success as art is entirely independent of its success in getting us to feel empathy or anything else. Something can get us to feel but be lousy art; or it can be great art but not get us to feel.

While Croce is worried about the aesthetic and moral problems of presenting unmediated or barely mediated suffering, other critics are worried about the aesthetic and moral problems of hypermediated portrayals of suffering. They are concerned that distancing of the very sort Croce seeks is precisely what makes artistic representations of suffering subject to close moral scrutiny. They may well agree with her that getting an audience to feel certain ways is not a sufficient condition of good art, but still insist—contra what may appear to be the upshot of #1 and #2—that, at least with certain genres of art, leading the audience to feel particular emotions is an important element of the goodness or the strength of the art. It is not at all unusual to find critics implying that art fails us, and fails us *aesthetically*, when, in the act of providing distance, art encourages sentimentality about or complacency in the face of human suffering; that art serves us when we are appropriately moved; and that—

contra #7—the distinction between good and great art sometimes turns (again, genre is important) on the skill the artist
employs in exemplifying that distinction.

For example, critics like Vicki Goldberg invite us to reflect
on the striking dissonance between highly virtuosic renderings
of the downtrodden and impoverished, and the conditions of
those living in such circumstances. In "Looking at the Poor in a
Gilded Frame," Goldberg surveys a number of photographs and
portraits of people living in poverty that were on display in gal-
leries across New York City in early 1995.[7] She reminds us that
critical responses to such exhibitions have always included worries about the possible abuse of those whose suffering occasions
the work of art. Jacob Riis's photographs of children and adults
living in extreme poverty run the risk of exemplifying "the sins
that documentary photography is heir to—its inclination to in-
trude, exploit, sensationalize, distance and patronize" (39).
Viewers are complicit in such "sins" to the extent that they convince themselves that they have gained the moral benefits of
learning how the other half lives without having to know any
such sufferers firsthand, without having any but their visual
sense (and that at secondhand) exposed to unspeakable living
conditions. In judging such works, Goldberg insists, we must
ask: Is human suffering being used simply as a pretext for the
artist's display of talent? Or perhaps as an opportunity for viewers to confirm that their compassion batteries are still charged?

Of course, as Goldberg points out, people don't need to have
direct exposure to poverty to do something about it, and photographs like Riis's sometimes do bring about social and economic change. But it is precisely because Goldberg is concerned

about such photographs as art and not merely as instruments of social change that she highlights the moral perils endemic to such portraiture.

There is a paradox here, one that has no room to emerge in an essay like Croce's. Goldberg does not judge portraits of poverty on the basis of whether viewing them leads audiences to engage in remedial action on behalf of the poor. (Although she does note that whether such portraits have this effect tends to depend on the larger artistic and social context: the more well known and densely remarked upon poverty is, the less impact representations of it are likely to have.) She assumes, however, that part of our assessment of the artistic value of such portraits involves how successfully they avoid and enable viewers to avoid certain moral compromises. For example: "do photographs in fine surroundings salve the conscience by stirring up just enough sympathy to assure us we have paid our emotional dues?" (1). Are audiences "paying lip service to compassion while hotly pursuing esthetics?" (39). Incorporating a phrase from Allan Sekula, Goldberg asks whether artists are using gorgeous representations of people in dire straits in " 'fetishistic cultivation' " of their own humanity (1). Goldberg presupposes that understanding the photographs is inseparable from asking these questions. We don't first have a complete description of the photographs, and then ask the questions; answering such questions is part of describing what is going on in the photographs.

As we saw, a key concept in Croce's analysis of the appropriate distance of art to suffering is transcendence. At the very least she seems to mean that if suffering is their topic, artists must do something with it; they can't simply parade it in front of the audience. Art that deals successfully with suffering, according to Croce, manages somehow to allude to suffering without getting lost in it and contains suffering in such a way that audiences do not have to feel that the only possible reaction is to feel sorry for the sufferers. What concerns Goldberg and the many critics she echoes is that, perhaps in response to something like #10, such transcendence all too often takes the form of making the art not about what it appears to be about—the impoverished child, the exploited worker—but functions instead to underscore the marvelous humanity of the artist, or to congratulate the viewer on her capacity to feel for the sufferer. The artwork transcends the condition of the sufferer by focusing, implicitly, on the condition of the artist or of the viewer.

Käthe Kollwitz apparently was preoccupied with the enormous power of art to transcend suffering in a related way; she was troubled by "the disturbing capability of art to elevate or beautify the unspeakable," to "transform ugly reality into something deceptively grand."[8] Indeed, some art critics have remarked upon what they consider to be Kollwitz's success in blocking the kind of suspect distance of which Goldberg and others have spoken. Here, for example, is Elizabeth Prelinger on Kollwitz's series of etchings and lithographs called collectively *A Weaver's Rebellion*: "By deliberately seeking a gritty and corroded surface of the plates she shaped the viewer's apprehension of the scene, removing the possibility of aestheticizing the event and forcing the beholder into the hovels of the destitute" (25). Commenting in more detail about the meaning of the works and the nature of the compassion encouraged, Linda Nochlin compares Kollwitz with Renouard, van Gogh, and Riis. The visual terms of Renouard's *Sans Travail*, like much of the work of van Gogh and Riis, express a kind of compassion that Nochlin refers to as "humanitarian": it "postulates the workers and the poor as victims" (10). But in *A Weaver's Rebellion*, on the other hand, we find the expression of what Nochlin terms a more "political" compassion, one that portrays the workers as "class-unified activists fighting for their rights by means of revolutionary, collective political action" (ibid.). In Kollwitz's hands, the weavers are portrayed as "downtrodden and starving" yet "making decisions and taking collective action against their oppressors"; they exhibit "a kind of desperate resolution rather than mere resignation" (114).

To take another example from Nochlin, this time from an essay on Leon Frédéric's *Grain* and *Flax* series on agricultural workers: like Millet and Breton, Nochlin claims, Frédéric "depicts . . . rural occupations as onerous, but rarely as painful"; unlike Kollwitz, but also even unlike van Gogh and Renouard, Frédéric seems to extoll rather than indict the social and economic system under which such work takes place (125); like Brueghel, Millet, and Monet, Frédéric is in the thrall of an "ideological structure . . . [that] associates the peasant with nature itself." He portrays workers as "unconscious instruments of inalterable processes, anonymous participants in unchanging rituals, rather than . . . rational beings living at specific historical moments with certain choices, prerogatives for change" (126). Nochlin's point is not that Frédéric had such specific intentions and managed to realize them in his paintings—she has nothing to say about his intentions. Her comments are about how close attention to Frédéric's use of his materials and to the details of the paintings reveal a fairly specific, even if unconscious, position about the meaning of such work and the nature of the burden it imposes on the workers.

Since Croce has made the intentions of artists so crucial to thinking about their work (see #1 and #2), it is worth noting that Lynn Garafola did not assess *Still/Here* on the basis of what she assumed ahead of time were its therapeutic aims, and her rather scathing critique of the piece makes no reference to these or any other intentions. Presumably, she didn't preclude the possibility that misguided intentions might help explain why the production, by her lights, ended up so disastrously, but viewed her job as that of commenting on the production, not unearthing those psychological states of the choreographer or dancers that threw them off the track artistically. The comments of critics like Vicki Goldberg and Linda Nochlin remind us that whatever the aims of Riis or Renouard or van Gogh or Millet or Frédéric or Kollwitz, the assessment of their works is based on the details in the works, not on the intentions of the artists—whatever role their intentions might have had in the complex production of their work (for example, the decision to use red, or the realization that what I've drawn is too much at odds with what I might roughly identify as what I was intending to do).

These brief dips into critical appraisals of artists such as Renouard, van Gogh, Riis, Kollwitz, and Frédéric alert us to the larger context in which Croce's views about the relation between art and human suffering sit. They remind us first of all that portrayals of human suffering are hardly uncommon in the arts. Such works of art cannot help but say something about the suffering they attempt to portray. They direct the viewer in how to think and feel about the nature of the suffering and the sufferers. (Of course, critics may disagree about just what those directions are. We needn't agree with the views of Goldberg or Prelinger or Nochlin, just note the terms of their assessments.) Are the sufferers depicted as mere victims, or as possible resisters, or sometimes even as collaborators? Is the viewer invited to be a mere spectator, or a potential actor? Asking such questions often is central to understanding and appraising a work of art. For instance, the rendering of facial expression, posture, hand position, focus of attention, choice of materials, style—all contribute to the production of the meaning of the artwork and to the response it is likely to induce.[9] Barry Schwabsky recently assessed the work of Jacob Lawrence along such lines: "After the mid-40's there is a tendency to abandon the eloquent reticence so evident in *The Migration* or in the *Harlem* series that logically followed enough in 1942–43, in favor of a more expressionistic style whose deformations reveal all too clearly their designs on the viewer's sympathies."[10]

Neither Goldberg, Prelinger, nor Nochlin is saying or even suggesting that the critical assessment of works of art dealing with suffering turns simply on the sense of whether it sends us the "right message" about such suffering. Nevertheless, the details of such criticism, and the critical appraisal of many others, including Arlene Croce, suggest that at least when it comes to works of art that purport to deal with human suffering, untangling aesthetic considerations from moral ones is out of the question (contra #7 and #8). This is not because artists are supposed to be producing artistic substitutes for moral treatises or preachy homilies, nor because critics are supposed to be dispensing or hoarding brownie points for good moral attitudes.

The unavoidable connection between aesthetic and moral considerations stems from the fact that it is impossible to make suffering your subject and not send a message—perhaps a quite complicated one—about its meaning. Or to put the point another way: even the hardiest champions of the art for art's sake school (Croce certainly seems to want to plant her flag here) would find it difficult to promise not to raise any morality-flavored questions about this kind of art. Should any critic make the following pledge? "Go ahead, make suffering your subject, but don't worry, I won't raise any questions—in my official capacity as critic, anyway—about whether your treatment is maudlin, or sentimental, or exploitative, or, on the other hand, appropriately sympathetic, or rigorously loving, or anything like that. I won't use any language at all that suggests that artist, audience, and critic have any moral burdens placed on them by art as such. I'll talk about your brush strokes, or your use of color, or your choreography, or the technical skills of your dancers, but I promise to do that without saying anything about the extent to which they serve or undermine your treatment of the suffering that is your subject. I promise not to look for anything in your art that might, oh, reveal more of an interest in glorifying the powers of the artist, or in congratulating the capacities of the audience, than in producing attention to the suffering that occasions the art."

Not all works of art have to do with human suffering; some don't have to do with anything at all—they aren't *about* anything (or maybe they aren't about anything except not being about anything). But artistic renderings of human suffering continue to be part of the various forms of art that surround us. Such works can't help but suggest a way of understanding and responding to the suffering depicted. Our reaction to them involves an assent to or resistance to such an understanding. The message of the work and our response to it are ripe for moral appraisal, a moral evaluation that is impossible to untangle from our aesthetic appraisal.

Once human suffering becomes the occasion for and topic of art, we cannot help but be on delicate moral ground. There are some situations in which we find ourselves, and transactions of which we are a part, such that we cannot bracket off from moral assessment what we think or feel or how we act. We certainly cannot claim such immunity simply on the grounds that we are working in or responding to a medium we call "art." So in thinking about the relation between art and suffering, this option is ruled out: I'll make art about suffering, but there will be no moral message, and it will not be appropriate for critics to be concerned about such a message.[11]

There is, of course, another option: to refuse to make art about suffering. This option has long been under serious consideration by those who wonder whether horrific suffering can be represented adequately at all, let alone by means of art. For example, is the Holocaust a "limit case of knowledge and feeling, in terms of which all . . . systems of belief and thought, all forms of literary and artistic expression seem irrelevant or even criminal"?[12] Not to try to represent it, however, seems out of the question, for at least two reasons. First, artistic silence invites charges of criminal neglect or implicit condonation. Second, there is a huge and ever-growing body of work providing witness to and depiction of the Holocaust. But the delicate and painful moral issues have not disappeared; they have only become more acute. Increasingly, information about and interpretations of the Holocaust are available, through university courses, museums and memorials, the various arts. There continues to be deep concern that all such activity is "a painful invasion of a private sphere, involving an unacceptable trivialization."[13] There is apprehension about an "unhealthy fascination with the Nazi era, a continuation . . . of the original hold that Hitler had upon his followers in times past"; distortions of fact seem inevitable, given the strength of "questionable literary or political purposes."[14] The scandalous possibility always exists of eroticizing or aestheticizing the slaughter of human beings.[15]

So the problems facing art critics when the art upon which they are commenting has suffering as its subject won't go away. But we are now in a position to see that in reflecting on such problems, some critics implicitly have come up with a credo considerably at odds with Croce's. Many critics no doubt would agree with Croce that thoughtful audiences will be alert to the possibility that a performance might simply be an excuse for a dose of psychological or political medicine. But these critics would also insist that such caution should not be confused with a refusal to consider what a work of art means in its social and political context, or with an insistence that judging it on its aesthetic merits is entirely separable from judging what it says or suggests to us. Otherwise Vicki Goldberg is entirely off the mark in asking us to think about what a photograph of extreme poverty suggests about the photographer's and the audience's relation to the scenes portrayed. Otherwise we must conclude that Linda Nochlin is out of bounds in her role as art critic in trying to tease out from the details of the painting what the message is about the meaning of endless toil. In fact, otherwise we must conclude that Croce's own comments on how some works of art successfully transcend suffering are off limits: she would have no business thinking about whether Keats or Schumann or Chopin or anyone else creates works of art that help us get the "right distance" from pain and suffering. Croce cannot really wish to cabin off art from the moral messages it sends; were she to do that, by her own reckoning she would make the critic "expendable." As critic, Croce relies on her moral judgment to tell us the difference between treatments of suffering that are matters of art and treatments that are not, and to mark the distinction between artistic treatments of suffering that achieve the right distance and those that do not.

Croce clearly is not alone in thinking that much rides on how we respond to suffering in the various dimensions of our lives. Let us now remind ourselves what others have thought is at stake.

SUFFERING AS THE HUMAN CONDITION

I

The sheer variety of writers whose work has been under scrutiny in this work—the differences among them in historical period, culture, and material circumstances—reminds us of the regularity with which we are called upon to respond to the human suffering around us. We have found most of these writers pressed into producing their own account of how to respond to suffering in the face of what they take to be dangerously wrong alternatives. Implicitly or explicitly, these writers propose that at least some small part of their world will be significantly better if the kind of suffering under examination is responded to as they suggest rather than as put forth in powerful competing accounts. The stakes are felt to be very high and the battle lines are drawn with considerable urgency.

For Plato, having the proper understanding of grief sepa-
rates the philosopher from both the poet who exploits grief and
the moral cynic who counsels avoiding it at all costs. The failure
of both poet and moral cynic to understand the causes and the
significance of human suffering is of a piece with their failure
to understand the nature of justice. Perhaps they have a strong
motivation not to understand it, Plato suggests, because in a
world ordered by the principles of justice laid out in the *Republic*, neither the poets nor a Thrasymachus will have an audience.
For in such a world there will be far fewer occasions for suffering, necessary grist for the poet's mill; and on such occasions as
do exist, the sorrow will be shared, and not, as Thrasymachus
taught, seen as something that is the inevitable lot of some because of the natural greed of others.

Harriet Jacobs lived in a world in which, of the competing
interpretations of the meaning of the suffering of slaves, those
proposed by slaves themselves carried no political weight, indeed, could barely be seen as alternatives to the views of slave
owners and their many supporters North and South. Because
Jacobs was so highly attuned to the interpretation of slaves'
suffering implicitly contained in a response of compassion, she
wanted both to invoke such compassion and to ensure that it
was a prelude to and not a substitute for the economic and political freedom she ardently desired and confidently claimed as
rightfully belonging to her and other slaves. Jacobs was aware
that people enjoying being in the saddle of compassion may
have disincentives to cancel the suffering that provides the ride.
She wanted to do what she could to ensure that the suffering of
slaves was ended, not simply eroded in the kind of piecemeal
fashion that continues to supply occasions for others to feel vir-

tuous. It is not that she didn't appreciate real compassion; but she was much more interested in the creation of opportunities for ex-slaves to exercise the virtues of citizenship than the continuation of opportunities for good Christians to exercise the virtues of compassion for the enslaved.

A common theme that emerges in these pages is that the means by which attention is brought to suffering may prolong or deepen rather than alleviate it, coupled with the assumption that competing views about how to respond to suffering may be judged by reference to this concern. Does referring to slavery as "the American tragedy" represent a recognition of the suffering of slaves, or does it instead add a hammer blow by finding something redeeming in the people or the system that produced such suffering? At what point or under what conditions does compassion become parasitical upon its suffering host? Does focusing on the importance of the cultivation of the capacity to care distract us from thinking about to whom the care is directed?

Some worries may seem more serious than others: grieving and having compassion appear to be at quite a remove from the wholesale appropriation of suffering that occurs when one group's experience of prolonged agony is noticed by another group only long enough to be adapted to its own ends. For example, having compassion for horribly overworked and underpaid children surely is different from using images of them to make profits for a clothing company. Moreover, it is hard to imagine that someone who really grieved over the lost youth or the early deaths of such children would use pictures of them to sell consumer goods. Grief over and compassion for the suffering of others seem to be not only different from the appropriation of the suffering but logically and psychologically incompatible with such appropriation. One cannot grieve unless one believes there is a serious loss and wishes that it had not happened; one cannot have compassion for someone unless one believes that the person is in an undesirable state and one wishes to alleviate it. While the profiteer may share the belief of the griever that there is a serious loss, and share the belief of the compassionate person that the sufferer is in an undesirable state,[1] the profiteer can't share the wish that the suffering hadn't happened or that it will end; for with the end of the suffering comes the surcease of profit.

Nevertheless, the concerns voiced in chapter 5 about the appropriation of suffering may illuminate the nature of Plato's worries involving the power of grief and Harriet Jacobs's concerns about the potential sloppiness of compassion. The suffering of one person may be the occasion for and original focus of another's grief or compassion, but the eye or the heart of the griever or compassionate person may all too easily roam. At least that seems to be a version of what Plato on the one hand and Jacobs on the other were worried about. For Plato grief ceases to serve whatever good purpose it has as soon as the griever grows more interested in prolonging the bittersweet sadness of his state than in focusing on how to properly understand and deal with the conditions that brought about the grievous situation. In his view, grief should function to register the weight of the loss incurred but instead it becomes a kind of psychic festering in the absence of attempts to take the proper measure of the weight, lift it, and think about how to prevent further occurrences of such loss. For Jacobs, compassion signals that one not only notices but also attends to the suffering in question. However, regarding compassion as a virtue is two-sided. On the one hand, as Jacobs assumed, it prompts those concerned with virtue to attune themselves to suffering they might not notice otherwise. On the other hand, the exercise of virtue may become desirable simply for its own sake—or rather for the sake of the person exercising it. The compassionate person's attention doesn't necessarily stay fixed on the object of her compassion and all too easily may roam toward herself as the subject, the person feeling the compassion—the place where Jacobs joins with Hannah Arendt in critically scrutinizing people whose interest in excelling at being empathetic or compassionate dwarfs careful solicitude for the objects of their care. Plato was alarmed by the pleasurable aspect of grieving, Jacobs by the pleasure in feeling compassion, in somewhat the same way those concerned with appropriation worry about profiteering in its various forms: whenever powerful forms of pleasure or satisfaction depend on the existence of suffering, attention to such suffering, however more desirable than inattention, carries with it the seeds of prolongation of that suffering. Plato and Jacobs wanted their audiences to consider the point at which the appetite for grieving or for feeling compassion becomes larger than the desire to do something useful for those who are the objects of their grief or compassion.

The point is not that Plato or Jacobs implies that each and every response to suffering ends up being a way of appropriating it, or that ultimately there is no difference between Benetton ads exploiting exploited children, AIDS victims referring to that horrible epidemic as another Holocaust, and someone grieving over or feeling compassion for a dying friend. To question whether a means of attending to the suffering of others carries the potential of a slide toward serving only one's own interests or enlarging one's own pleasures doesn't mean that this shift will happen. On the contrary, many of the writers I've referred to are vociferous about their own proposals precisely because they wish to avoid such a shift and they think their competitors don't recognize the problem.

Both Plato and Croce regard theater as a particularly powerful means of bringing attention to suffering and of themselves as watchful guardians over the lessons about suffering that appear on the stage—Plato in the name of philosophy, Croce in the name of art. Plato is quite certain that there is no way for the tragic theater to avoid sending the wrong message about the place of grief in human life, and that it is more important for the citizens of Greece to get grief right than for the tragic theater (or anything similar that might succeed it) to continue. Croce, on the other hand, is quite confident that the means exist for dance and other art forms to deal appropriately with suffering, but that employing these means requires keeping a clear distinction between performances for politics' sake and performances for art's sake, or between parading sufferers on stage and portraying them. She seems to think that while it would be a mistake to regard art as existing *in order* to get the right distance from suffering, art, properly understood, can provide that distance. But it cannot supply this distance if it generates compassion for real sufferers on stage, for if that is what is going on, there is no art, whatever else is being accomplished. In this sense Croce implies that the kind of aesthetic distance from suffering that art provides brings with it a moral bonus: in providing a way to transcend the suffering it portrays, art suggests avenues out of suffering that are morally superior to what she considers self-indulgent wallowing. Implicit in Croce's critique of the Bill T. Jones piece that she did not see is the view that bad art about suffering gives us both a politically pernicious view about art and a morally pernicious view about suffering.

A little earlier I suggested that there seemed to be a shared worry among many of our writers that the means by which attention is brought to suffering may prolong or deepen rather than alleviate it, and a shared sense that competing views are to be judged by reference to this worry. This doesn't quite describe Croce's central concern, which is less about what happens to the suffering responded to than about what happens to the means by which attention is brought to it. In her view, performers and audiences who don't understand the proper relationship between art and suffering threaten to contaminate art.

The stakes, then, in these micro-battles over the most appropriate way to respond to suffering are presented as being very high. Will it be the way of the philosophers, or of the poets? Will we be guided by the constraints of Platonic justice, or the insatiability of grief? Whose views about the suffering of slaves will be heard—those of the slaves themselves, or their slave owners and the ministers, doctors, and politicians who support them? Will there be real compassion for the slaves, or dehumanizing reduction of them to victims? Will compassion for slaves blot out or substitute for anger at the slave owners? Will the suffering of one part of humanity be used respectfully and carefully by others, or treated as recyclable experience, open to any use deemed suitable by the new owners? Will we have Crocean-approved artists, or a swarmy parade of wallowing victims?

II

In the process of trying to alert us to what is at stake in getting the right take on suffering, many of our writers also implicitly produce accounts of who is likely to understand suffering, who is not, and why. Who, if anyone, has the requisite authority and expertise about suffering? How are we to recognize such qualities?

To the Plato of the *Republic*, people in the throes of grief are least likely to understand, indeed to want to understand, the causes of their suffering. Only those philosopher-kings and -queens not themselves subject to the enticements of grieving know how to respond properly to the conditions producing the grievous situations. In less than perfect polities, these conditions include such things as the creations of Homer and the tragedians, who only know enough about grief to be able to whet our voracious appetite for it. The real experts on understanding suffering, not on producing it, are the philosophers.

For Aristotle, philosophers also are the experts on suffering, not because they have learned not to be enticed by grief, but because they are in a position to pass judgment on the appropriateness of tragedy's showing us whose suffering is tragic and whose is not. Good tragedy instructs correctly about suffering, but philosophers get to tell us what is good tragedy and what is not.

Harriet Jacobs hoped to undercut the authority over the meaning of the suffering of slaves invested in the very people causing or sustaining it. She was concerned that the arguments or assumptions about slaves' lack of full humanity would also be used to ignore or discount what slaves themselves had to say about the suffering they endured. She did not argue that slaves had an unchallengeable claim to know best how to respond to their suffering, only that their views must be considered. In this sense she was more interested in dislodging certain groups of people as experts on the meaning of the suffering of slaves than in installing another group as final, irrefutable authorities.

Hannah Arendt's work suggests that she sees grave dangers in making anybody an expert on suffering. She presents Robespierre as a case study in why we should be deeply skeptical of anyone proclaiming to understand and know how to respond to the suffering of other people. Her embrace of what she refers to as compassionate cosuffering implies that we are all equally expert in knowing how best to respond to suffering to the extent that we are capable of a perspectiveless cofeeling with others. (Of course, to announce that there are no experts presumes expertise of some sort. But in this sense not just Arendt presents herself as an expert.)

In this connection there are Arendtian contours to concerns about the possibility of exploitatively appropriating the suffering of others in order to bring attention to our own. The more assuredly we present ourselves as enduring what others have experienced, the more expertise we implicitly assume as interpreters of their suffering and of their sense of appropriate responses to it. This is why, for example, the assertion by white women in mid-nineteenth-century America that they were slaves was an exhibition of their relative power in a society whose major institutions sustained ideologies not only of sexual but of "racial" supremacy. The authority that white women claimed about the meaning of the suffering of slaves is not something they thought slaves had about the suffering of being women. To put on the mantle of others' suffering is to proclaim oneself as well informed (even if not an expert) about what that suffering means. That is one of the reasons why any of us inclined to invoke the Holocaust to bring attention to other examples of humanity's horrors ought to be prepared to defend our implicit claim to being well informed about the meaning of that particular event.

Arlene Croce implies that in good art we have vouchsaved for us not the only but certainly an important means for understanding suffering: good art is distinguished from bad art by achieving the right distance from it. Art does not exist in order to render this possible but its existence turns out to make such distance possible. However, artists are not necessarily the ultimate experts about what this distance is. Just as Aristotle implied that philosophers decide what is good tragedy and what isn't, Croce implies that the critic gets to decide what is good dance and what isn't. So it is the critic who is the ultimate arbiter of what defines the right distance between art and the suffering that it sometimes portrays.

III

This book began with a reminder of how saturated our every-day lives are with judgments about suffering and with conceptual tools to sort out and make sense of it. Not included in that brief opening catalog was the category of commonplaces about suffering, grand statements about its place in human life. One of the most familiar is that suffering is the human condition. Whether such a claim ends up being a hiccup at the end of an inspirational speech or a hint of a profound truth depends upon what it is supposed to mean. None of the writers populating these pages offers direct clarification, affirmation, or denial of the idea that suffering is the human condition. But they leave us with several ways of understanding that familiar and frustratingly vague proposition and with the unfinished but highly suggestive task of thinking about the implications of each formulation.

Version A: Suffering is the human condition in the sense that those whose suffering we take seriously are those whose humanity we take seriously and vice versa.

This way of connecting one's status as a human and as a sufferer was particularly vivid in the discussion in chapter 2 of the ineligibility of the Aristotelian slave—by "nature" not fully human—to assume the status of tragic hero. It appeared in Linda Brent's concern that the suffering of slaves would not be acknowledged, or acknowledged only long enough for "good Christians" to feel virtuous affirmation of their own superior humanity. It was echoed in Hannah Arendt's anxiety about pity's assertion of the lesser human status of its object. It lies behind the concern voiced in chapter 4 about the absence of attention to the question of who becomes the object of care. It is expressed in chapter 5's scrutiny of the difference between using someone else's experience of suffering as a way of affirming a sense of shared humanity, and simply profiting from others' history of being treated as if they were not fully human.

Version B: Suffering is the human condition in the sense that an important sign of acknowledging the full humanity of others and of taking their suffering seriously is the willingness to consider their view of what that suffering means.

Harriet Jacobs clearly wanted her voice as a female slave to be heard for several reasons: to provide an accurate view of what slavery entailed; to establish her presence as someone who had not been and would not be reduced to the status of a passive voiceless victim; and to ensure that the focus on the suffering of slavery includes those who are responsible for it, not just those who endure its horrors (her concern about the denial of her full humanity is linked with her insistence on the right to comment on the inhumanity of others). The significance of the sufferers' own views was a prominent theme in reflections on the possibility that an empathetic identification with others' suffering may be a way of silencing them and making yourself their ventriloquist. Finally, questions about the appropriation of others' experience of suffering suggested that we have reason to be suspicious of one person's borrowing the history of your suffering to make sense of her own, if she has no interest in finding out what the "lender" has to say about the proposed comparison.

Version C: Suffering is the human condition in the sense that it is by reference to suffering that crucial differences among humans are articulated.

Humans have in common the fact that they suffer and that they are called upon to respond to suffering. But like so much else that humans can be said to share, what they have in common can be used either to mark ways in which they are the same, or provide the means by which to mark significant distinctions among them. To take an invidious example, unless it were believed to be the case that all humans have "racial" characteristics, there would be no way to compare or contrast people "racially."

In the case of both Plato and Aristotle, it is particularly clear that their views about suffering are intimately tied to their hierarchical ranking of persons or polities. They suggest that suffering, and responding to it, are so much the human condition that significant differences among humans are echoed in exemplary differences in their suffering or in their responses to it.

For example, one way in which Plato thought philosophy could and should make its distinctive mark is by having a view about the causes and significance of suffering superior to what he saw offered by Greek culture. We are supposed to learn from the *Republic* that part of the superiority of male and female leaders of the ideal polis is that they are never overwhelmed by grief, that they are rulers in a society where the occasions for tragic suffering are diminished by proper political organization. (Such a view is no doubt part of what Nietzsche so vehemently railed against in his tirades against Socratic "optimism" and "cheerfulness.") Thus both the liability to suffering, and the disposition to grieve, are treated as markers of the inferiority of some polities to others and of some types of human constitutions to others.

Though Aristotle was happy to entertain a much more robust role for the tragic theater than was Plato, and seemed to be less anxious than his teacher about the bloating effects of grief, he invites us to make significant distinctions between human groups by reference to the usefulness of their suffering: only the suffering of some kinds of people has the capacity to instruct and move its audience in ways that entitle such suffering to be considered tragic. This distinction corresponds neatly to the fundamental difference Aristotle sees between the basic natures of citizens and slaves.

In their discussions of tragedy and grief, Plato and Aristotle thus underwrite a political economy of suffering—a distribution of attention that articulates remarkably neatly with their views about the appropriate political hierarchy of persons. Indications of a political economy of compassion also have appeared in these pages, but most often in a variety of attempts not to underwrite but to question it.

As a precious human resource, the distribution of compassion is likely to be regulated, and such regulation, which encompasses not only who gets the goods but who delivers them, is not likely to be neutral with respect to the distribution of other resources in a society. As we learn from some late-twentieth-century feminists, we ought to inquire about any given society at any given moment whether it falls to some rather than others to do the work of care and compassion, and what kind of social, economic, and political standing attaches to such division of labor.[2] We also can ask, following the lead of Harriet Jacobs, when care and compassion for those systematically exploited or discriminated against tend to subvert or on the contrary to sustain the ideological mechanisms and social institutions meant to keep them in their place.

> *Version D: Suffering is the human condition in the sense that the experiences of suffering of some can be put to good use by others, despite what would appear to be significant differences among them. Whatever benefits may be extracted from particular forms of suffering need not be regarded as belonging only to those who have endured them.*

How we conceive of this stored-up supply of human suffering—in this view our human condition—has much to do with how the benefits and burdens of suffering are thought to be distributed.

On the one hand, suffering might be treated as so common that all of us can be seen both as potential contributors to and potential borrowers from a bank of shared human experience of suffering. Against the background of a refusal to see some people's suffering as instructive or usable for one's own (see chapters 2 and 5), such a picture of shared humanity might help rot away the underpinnings of claims to "racial," ethnic, or other kinds of superiority. Not only do all of us suffer, but our suffering is similar to the extent that what one person or group contributes to the pool of human experience can be drawn from for use by another person or group. Under the sway of such a metaphor—and revealing what lies at its troubling limits—the blood that Black women and men shed under slavery might be thought of as providing a transfusion for disfranchised white women, the horrors of the Holocaust as reconstituted or reconfigured for the use of AIDS victims.

I am not suggesting that anyone has actually extended the bank metaphor this far or in these particular ways (though in this context we might be more tempted than ever to think of some advertisers as bloodsuckers). Seeing this metaphor pushed to its limits is likely to make many of us acutely uncomfortable, especially should it begin to look as if some people are allowed only to make deposits, others expected only to make withdrawals.

At this point the bank metaphor appears to become transformed into one that suggests we think of human suffering not as a storehouse but as an arable field, on which some do the difficult work of plowing and planting, and others arrive just in time to enjoy the harvest. This metaphor highlights the ambivalence humans seem to have about suffering: it is dirty work, but sometimes there are spiritual profits to be gained. Like so much else of the housework of humanity, we're not at all sure that the benefits that might accrue to us from its existence require us to do the actual work. Sometimes the use of other people's experience of suffering to make sense of our own turns out to be a way to exploit their labor: I acknowledge your suffering only to the extent to which it promises to bring attention to my own. You sow the seeds, I pluck the fruits of sorrow.

Introduction

1. This is an expression used in a slightly different context by my mother, Elizabeth S. Spelman (1911–1974), to whom this book is dedicated.

2. As Susan Sontag has demonstrated, some such judgments are packed into the metaphors that have powerfully shaped our understanding of tuberculosis, cancer, and AIDS. See *Illness as Metaphor* and *Aids and Its Metaphors*, published as one volume by Penguin (London, 1991).

3. See René Descartes, *Meditations*, VI: "All these sensations of hunger, thirst, pain, etc. are in truth none other than certain confused modes of thought which are produced by the union and apparent intermingling of mind and body." *The Essential Descartes*, ed. Margaret D. Wilson (New York: Mentor, 1969), 216.

4. Elaine Scarry, *The Body in Pain: The Making and Unmaking of the World* (New York: Oxford University Press, 1985).

5. See, for example, Raymond Williams, *Modern Tragedy* (Stanford: Stanford University Press, 1966).

6. I say "relatively" equal because accidents of birth as well as social and political institutions influence our vulnerability to suffering and our expectation of resources to deal with it. At the same time, we ought to ask

when what are called "accidents of birth" are themselves traceable to existing distribution of resources.

7. See Martin Pernick, *A Calculus of Suffering: Pain, Professionalism, and Anesthesia in Nineteenth-Century America* (New York: Columbia University Press, 1985).

8. The point I wish to make here depends on a thoroughly uncontroversial use of the concept of "art." Those interested in battles over what does and does not count as art may find some titillation if not illumination in chapter 6.

9. Some exceptions to this apparent pattern can be located by looking for caucus sessions at meetings of the American Philosophical Association, or course offerings at the margins of philosophy departments.

10. We should remember that Plato apparently found it convenient not to think explicitly about forms of suffering entailed by the institution of slavery.

Chapter One

1. See *Phaedo* 60b. Citations to Plato's works will be made parenthetically in the text. References are to *Gorgias*, trans. W. D. Woodhead; *Phaedo*, trans. H. Tredenick; and *Republic*, trans. P. Shorey, in *The Collected Dialogues*, ed. Edith Hamilton and Huntington Cairns (New York: Bollingen Foundation, 1961).

2. Though the Greek *lupe* can mean pain of either body or mind, Plato uses it frequently in the *Republic* to refer to a psychological capacity.

3. Book 10's analysis of poetry as *mimēsis* and its effects on the soul differs rather wildly from that given in books 2 and 3—in particular with respect to how much poetry is mimetic, what *mimēsis* is, and just how it appeals to the "baser" parts of the soul. For a helpful summary of these

174

differences, see Julia Annas, *An Introduction to Plato's Republic* (New York: Oxford University Press, 1981), 336–344.

4. Plato often has been criticized for failing to appreciate audiences' abilities to distinguish between what is represented on a stage and what occurs in real life. For a particularly helpful examination of this criticism, see Alexander Nehamas, "Plato and the Mass Media," *Monist* 71 (1988): 214–234.

5. If, along with Terence Irwin, we take it to be characteristic of the "spirited" part of the soul (*thumoeides*) that it "has evaluative attitudes, resting on some belief about the goodness or badness of its object," grief would appear to belong to the spirit, since it is constituted in part by a belief that someone or something valuable has been lost (Terence Irwin, *Plato's Ethics* [New York: Oxford University Press, 1995], 212). On the other hand, if, following Thomas Gould, we focus on passages such as 606a (about the part of the soul that has "hungered to lament and to get enough grieving and to be satiated, it being its nature to yearn for these things" [Gould's translation]), we are reminded that sometimes Plato explicitly locates grief in the appetitive aspect of the soul (*epithymētikon*). Indeed, Gould seems to have no doubt that the correct way to describe Plato's central concern about the poets is that they "have nothing to say to the rational element in our souls, or to its angry ally, the middle part. They appeal only to the lowest element in our beings," that is, our appetites (Thomas Gould, *The Ancient Quarrel between Poetry and Philosophy* [Princeton: Princeton University Press, 1990], 31, 33).

6. Socrates appears to contradict himself here: if we can't really know what is good and evil, how can we know that nothing in our mortal life is worthy of concern? Perhaps his point is that to grieve is to assume without question that the loss is not good and that it keeps one from thinking about what would be best to do in light of the loss. (Of course to exculpate Socrates from self-contradiction is not necessarily to agree with him about the substantive claims.)

7. The point of this chapter—to which we shall return briefly in the conclusion—is not to figure out whether Plato was right about grief, psy-

chologically, ethically, or politically, but rather to explore why he thought it so important to get grief right. Clearly, many commentators, and not just late-twentieth-century experts in grieving, would disagree with Plato's claim here: they would insist that on the contrary, unless and until we grieve, we cannot think carefully about the situation.

8. Indeed, the justice of the state depends on the justice, and the happiness, of each of its members. The state cannot be just unless all members perform the kind of task that is appropriate for them by reason of their natural capacities, and these citizens will not be able to perform such tasks well unless they have the appropriate harmony and unity of reason, spirit, and appetite.

9. On the engagement of Plato with many of the issues central to the tragedies, Martha Nussbaum remarks: "Far from having forgotten about what tragedy describes, he sees the problems of exposure so clearly that only a radical solution seems adequate to their depth." *The Fragility of Goodness: Luck and Ethics in Greek Tragedy and Philosophy* (Cambridge: Cambridge University Press, 1986), 18.

10. Although Plato's views about grief are not reducible to his views about gender traits and gender relations, neither are they fully understandable without them. Nor is any examination of Plato's views about women complete without an exploration of his views about grief. See, for example, Arlene W. Saxenhouse, "The Philosopher and the Female in the Political Thought of Plato," in *Feminist Interpretations of Plato*, ed. Nancy Tuana (University Park: Pennsylvania State University Press, 1994), 68; Nussbaum, 131, 230. The analysis here differs from Nussbaum's in locating the *Republic*'s treatment of grief not only in the context of its attack on tragedy but also in relation to Socrates' response to Thrasymachus.

11. Nussbaum, 18.

12. For a helpful discussion of the role of the division of labor in Plato's notion of justice, see Annas, *Introduction*, 109–152.

13. For close readings and very helpful suggestions, many thanks to Susan Levin, Helen Longino, Diana Tietjens Meyers, Martha Minow, and skeptical audiences at Miami University, Hartwick College, and the Canadian Society for Women in Philosophy.

Chapter Two

1. I am suggesting that this characterizes tragedy, even though, of course, the definition of what counts as tragedy changes. See, for example, Raymond Williams, *Modern Tragedy* (Stanford: Stanford University Press, 1966).

2. Audre Lorde, *Sister Outsider* (Trumansburg, N.Y.: Crossing Press, 1984), 171.

3. For a particularly enlightening analysis of the history and meaning of this comparison, see Jean Fagan Yellin, *Women and Sisters: The Antislavery Feminists in American Culture* (New Haven: Yale University Press, 1989). Yellin's book is discussed in chapter 5.

4. For example: "We may confidently assert that many of the aesthetic problems which have been since raised never even occurred to his mind, though precise answers to almost all such questions have been extracted from his writings by the unwise zeal of his admirers" (*Aristotle's Theory of Poetry and Fine Art*, ed. S. H. Butcher [New York: Dover, 1951; reprint, 1911 edition of 1894 translation], 113–114). "While, of course, this is not the only ancient text to be subjected to a series of misapplications, temporary, local, and mutually inconsistent, the *Poetics* must be distinguished by almost total failure of contact between Aristotle's argument and the successive traditions of exegesis" (John Jones, *On Aristotle and Greek Tragedy* [Stanford: Stanford University Press, 1962], 11). "For despite the thousands of pages that have been written on this notion [*hamartia*], we still need an account that is fully responsive to the ways in which, for Aristotle, practical error can come about through some

causes other than viciousness of character and still matter to the value of a life" (Martha C. Nussbaum, *The Fragility of Goodness: Luck and Ethics in Greek Tragedy and Philosophy* [Cambridge: Cambridge University Press, 1986], 382).

5. *Poetics* 1449b24–28, trans. Ingram Bywater, in *The Complete Works of Aristotle*, Vol. 2, ed. Jonathan Barnes (Princeton: Princeton University Press, 1984).

6. In much of the *Poetics* Aristotle speaks as if pity and fear in the combination necessary for the tragic effect will, in fact, occur if and only if certain things are true about the characters and events involved. But since elsewhere—particularly in the *Nicomachean Ethics*—Aristotle insists that it is difficult to feel the right thing in the right way in the right amount toward the right person or thing, it is hard to imagine that he rules out the possibility that members of the audience of a good tragedy might fail to feel what they are supposed to. They might, for example, pity those they shouldn't, fail to pity those they should, and so forth. A good tragedy does not just plug into emotions we already have; it also instructs us about how to feel.

7. *Poetics* 1453a6–12, 14–17.

8. *Poetics* 1454b8–9.

9. We can talk this way without forgetting that for Aristotle agents are carriers of action rather than action being the showcase for agents. "Tragedy is essentially an imitation not of persons but of action and life" (*Poetics* 1450a16).

10. John Kekes, *Facing Evil* (Princeton: Princeton University Press, 1990), 34.

11. *Poetics* 1451a37–38.

12. *Poetics* 1451b5–9. No doubt one of the reasons why we twentieth-century readers have a hard time understanding just what *mimēsis* or (roughly) "imitation," means is that given what we typically mean by "imitation"

it is difficult to imagine what imitating something described as universal could be.

13. Or anyway those who Aristotle thought to be the audience for tragedy. Gassner is no doubt right in saying that "Aristotle measures the effects of art with reference to reasonable men rather than lunatics, grown-up men rather than infants, and men capable of sympathy rather than inveterate sadists" (John Gassner, "Aristotelian Literary Criticism," introductory essay to *Aristotle's Theory of Poetry and Fine Art*, ed. S. H. Butcher [New York: Dover, 1951], xliii). But Gassner doesn't consider whether Aristotle would have included free women and male and female slaves among those "reasonable men" in the audience.

14. Aristotle, *Nicomachean Ethics* 1104b12–13, trans. W. D. Ross, in Barnes, *Complete Works*, op. cit. Aristotle says he is simply repeating here what he learned from Plato.

15. *Nicomachean Ethics* 1125b32–34.

16. *Republic* 605b–d. See chapter 1.

17. Nussbaum, 385.

18. Robert C. Solomon, *The Passions: The Myth and Nature of Human Emotion* (Garden City, N.Y.: Anchor-Doubleday, 1977), 139 ff.

19. Nussbaum, 391.

20. For a review of such differences and their significance, see my *Inessential Woman: Problems of Exclusion in Feminist Thought* (Boston: Beacon Press, 1988), especially chapter 2.

21. See *History of Animals*, 518a27 ff., 548a23 ff., 550a17 ff.

22. See, for example, *Poetics* 1454a21, in which Aristotle allows that "goodness is possible in every type of personage, even in a woman or a slave,

though the one is perhaps an inferior, and the other a wholly worthless being."

23. *Poetics* 1453a7–8, 1454b8.

24. *Poetics* 1453a3–4.

25. *Politics* 1255a6, trans. Benjamin Jowett, in Barnes, *Complete Works*, op. cit.

26. See *Politics* 1254b20 ff., 1260a12–13.

27. *Poetics* 1454a20. For a discussion of the apparent disjunction "woman or slave" in Aristotle, see my *Inessential Woman*, 37–50 and passim.

28. *Poetics* 1454a21.

29. *Politics* 1278a3 ff.

30. See *Nicomachean Ethics* 1103a5.

31. *Politics* 1260a34–36.

32. Unless, perhaps, the state you are born into is an indication of the kind of life you led in an earlier incarnation. On such a possibility, see Plato, *Republic* 613e ff.; *Laws* 944e; *Timaeus* 42b–c, 91a.

33. In *Moral Luck*, Bernard Williams distinguishes between "incident luck" and "constitutive luck" to mark the difference between what may happen to one in the course of a lifetime, and the conditions of the state into which one is born (Cambridge: Cambridge University Press, 1981), 20.

34. See, for example, *Politics* 1255b35–36, 1273a32 ff., 1277b6.

35. *Politics* 1259b36–38.

36. John Gassner, "Aristotelian Literary Criticism," introductory essay to *Aristotle's Theory of Poetry and Fine Art*, ed. S. H. Butcher, xliii.

37. Gassner, xlii.

38. Nussbaum, 382.

39. Butcher, 237.

40. Orlando Patterson, *Slavery and Social Death: A Comparative Study* (Cambridge: Harvard University Press, 1982). The "social death" of slaves has to do with "the permanent, violent domination of natally alienated and generally dishonored persons" (13). Denied connection by birth to any social order, slaves remain powerless and dishonored.

41. See my *Inessential Woman*, 37–50.

42. For a sustained discussion, see Wayne Booth, *The Company We Keep: The Ethics of Fiction* (Berkeley: University of California Press, 1988), 3–5, 457–478.

43. For a discussion of the ways in which Aristotle was invoked in the defense of American slavery, see Mavis Campbell, "Aristotle and Black Slavery: A Study in Race Prejudice," *Race* 15, no. 3 (1974): 283–301.

44. Mark Twain, *The Adventures of Huckleberry Finn* (New York: Bantam, 1985; originally published, 1884), 213.

45. George M. Frederickson, *The Black Image in the White Mind: The Debate on Afro-American Character and Destiny* (New York: Harper & Row, 1971), 57–58. See also Martin Pernick, *A Calculus of Suffering: Pain, Professionalism, and Anesthesia in Nineteenth-Century America* (New York: Columbia University Press, 1985), 154–167.

46. Carter G. Woodson, *Mississippi Valley Historical Review* 5 (March 1919), 480, 481. As quoted in *Black History and the Historical Profession, 1915–*

1980, by August Meier and Elliot Rudwick (Urbana: University of Illinois Press, 1986), 4, 98.

47. Meier and Rudwick, 239 ff.

48. Frederickson, xiii.

49. David Brion Davis, *The Problem of Slavery in the Age of Revolution, 1770– 1823* (Ithaca: Cornell University Press, 1975), 260, quoting Edmund S. Morgan, "Slavery and Freedom: The American Paradox," *Journal of American History* 59 (June 1972): 6. On page 261 Davis adds: "Eighteenth-century southern leaders could promote the ideal of a free white yeomanry and profess allegiance to the rights of all Englishmen precisely because black slaves had taken the place of a lower caste of whites."

50. Davis, 286.

51. As Molly Shanley has reminded me, a reference to slavery as *the* American tragedy entirely ignores the question of white settlers' treatment of those peoples already inhabiting the land.

52. Patterson, ix.

53. Claude G. Bowers, *The Tragic Era: The Revolution after Lincoln* (Cambridge: Houghton Mifflin, 1929), 218. Eric Foner has described Bowers's book as a "national bestseller" that popularized a "rewriting of Reconstruction's history" by a circle of professional historians whose work has been the source of "everlasting shame" to the profession (*A Short History of Reconstruction, 1863–1877* [New York: Harper & Row, 1990], 258).

54. He cannot know, given what he knows otherwise at the time, and given the element of surprise that, according to Aristotle, is important to good tragedy. *Poetics* 1452a4.

55. In this connection, see Aristotle's *Nicomachean Ethics* 1110b19 ff.: "Of people, then, who act by reason of ignorance he who regrets is thought an involuntary agent."

56. Sophocles, *Oedipus Rex*. *The Oedipus Cycle*, English versions by Dudley Fitts and Robert Fitzgerald (New York: Harcourt, Brace & World, 1939), 70, 71, 72 (lines 1330–1333, 1369–1370, 1414–1415). One can't help but be reminded of Socrates' extended reply throughout the *Republic* to the question raised first by Thrasymachus at 344c–d about whether one ought to fear doing wrong more than suffering it.

57. Peter J. Parish, *Slavery: History and Historians* (New York: Harper & Row, 1989), 3.

58. Parish, 3, 9, 10, 125, 132.

59. James Oakes, *The Ruling Race: A History of American Slaveholders* (New York: 1982), 121. As quoted in Parish, 139.

60. Oakes, 102–103. As quoted in Parish, 53.

61. Frederick Douglass, *The Constitution of the United States: Is It Pro-Slavery or Anti-Slavery?* (Halifax: T. & W. Birtwhistle, 1860), 14. Reprinted in *The Antislavery Argument*, ed. William H. Pease and Jane H. Pease (Indianapolis: Bobbs-Merrill, 1965), 356.

62. James Baldwin, *The Fire Next Time* (New York: Dell, 1962), 35.

63. Baldwin, 77, 79.

64. In a related context Carolyn Kay Steedman has written about the failure of many writers on the lives of working-class people to look for interesting and complicated textures in the consciousnesses of their subjects. See her *Landscape for a Good Woman* (New Brunswick, N.J.: Rutgers University Press, 1987), 13 ff. and passim.

65. W. E. B. Du Bois, *The Souls of Black Folk*, in *Three Negro Classics* (New York: Avon, 1965), 216. For a suggestion of the ways in which spiritual quests, whatever suffering they involve, are not tragic, see Iris Murdoch, *The Unicorn* (New York: Avon, 1963), 285 and passim.

183

66. Lawrence W. Levine, *Black Culture and Black Consciousness: Afro-American Folk Thought from Slavery to Freedom* (New York: Oxford University Press, 1977), 37.

67. Du Bois, 344.

68. Many thanks to Roger Gottlieb for the invitation to contribute to a volume honoring Richard Schmitt; to Richard Schmitt for the inspiration; to Martha Minow for incisive comments along the way; and to inquisitive audiences at Siena College and Dalhousie University.

Chapter Three

1. *Incidents in the Life of a Slave Girl, Written by Herself* [1861], ed. Jean Fagan Yellin (Cambridge: Harvard University Press, 1987), 29–30.

2. Angelina Grimké, letter 17 to Catharine Beecher, in *The Public Years of Sarah and Angeline Grimké: Selected Writings 1835–1839*, ed. Larry Ceplain (New York: Columbia University Press, 1989), 171. Emphasis in the original.

3. Frances Ellen Watkins Harper, address, "Duty to Dependent Races," National Council of Women of the United States, *Transactions* (Philadelphia, 1891), 86. As quoted in *Black Women in Nineteenth-Century American Life*, ed. Bert James Loewenberg and Ruth Bogin (University Park: Pennsylvania State University Press, 1976), 247.

4. "Introduction: Meditations on History: The Slave Woman's Voice," in *Invented Lives: Narratives of Black Women 1860–1960*, ed. Mary Helen Washington (Garden City, N.Y.: Doubleday-Anchor, 1987), 8.

5. Hannah Arendt, *The Human Condition* (Garden City, N.Y.: Doubleday-Anchor, 1959), 46. Future references to this work in the text will be designated by *HC* and page number.

6. Hannah Arendt, *On Revolution* (New York: Penguin, 1977), 60 ff. References to this work in the text will be designated by *OR* and page number.

7. Yet she also wonders, along the lines of Cicero, whether human beings are "so shabby that they are incapable of acting humanly unless spurred and as it were compelled by their own pain when they see others suffer." "On Humanity in Dark Times: Thoughts about Lessing," in her *Men in Dark Times* (New York: Harcourt, Brace & World, 1968), 15.

8. Here Arendt differs from those who see real compassion as characterized by an inclination to action. See, for example, Lawrence Blum, "Compassion," in *Explaining Emotions*, ed. Amélie Oksenberg Rorty (Berkeley: University of California Press, 1980).

9. According to Arendt (*OR*, 85), compassion, as a passion and thus different from reason, knows nothing of the general and "can only comprehend the particular"; the cosuffering involved in compassion is something one cannot do with more than a person at a time. As we shall see later in this chapter, Harriet Jacobs appeared to differ with Arendt on both these points.

10. Arendt does not seem here to reflect on those occasions when we do have doubts about whether someone is really in pain or are uncertain what their pain means. Though she certainly must have been aware of debates over the meaning of a person's or a group's suffering, she does not seem to regard those as having anything to do with emotion.

11. See, for example, Karl Morrison, *"I Am You": The Hermeneutics of Empathy in Western Literature, Theology, and Art* (Princeton: Princeton University Press, 1988). See chapter 5.

12. For some useful and telling criticisms of Arendt's account of the participants in the French Revolution, the kinds of activities they engaged in, and the framework Arendt employs in drawing sharp distinctions between the French and American Revolutions, see Joan Landes, *"Novus Ordo Saec[u]lorum*: Gender and Public Space in Arendt's Revolutionary

France," in *Feminist Interpretations of Hannah Arendt*, ed. Bonnie Honig (University Park: Pennsylvania State University Press, 1995), 195–219.

13. *Incidents*. Page references in this section are to this text.

14. Harriet Jacobs used the pseudonym Linda Brent no doubt for a variety of reasons, among them the desire to preserve the anonymity of Blacks and whites who had helped her. I shall refer to the main character of *Incidents* just as Jacobs did—as Linda Brent.

15. Though of course greatly relieved finally to be free, Brent rankles at the thought that her own freedom had to be *purchased*: "being sold from one owner to another seemed too much like slavery" (199).

16. "I do earnestly desire to arouse the women of the North to a realizing sense of the condition of two millions of women at the South, still in bondage, suffering what I suffered, and most of them far worse" (1). The rest of *Incidents* makes clear that it was to their virtues as Christian women, particularly Christian mothers, that Brent especially appealed. As Frances Smith Foster has pointed out to me, Jacobs's work dates from a time in her life when she was nominally free and actively engaged in abolitionist activity not only with whites but with other free Blacks (for example, she and her brother ran an abolitionist reading room in Rochester, New York). She knew her work was likely to be read by other exslaves, who were an implicit if not explicit audience.

17. There were, of course, different abolitionist camps, but distinguishing among them is not a major concern of Brent here.

18. Linda Brent indicates in a variety of ways the limitations on the slaves' knowledge of their own and other slaves' experiences. In the context of commenting on to what extent the brutality of slavery blunted slaves' awareness of "the humiliation of their position," she includes herself among those who, precisely because they were so aware of what they went through, "cannot tell how much" they actually suffered nor how much they are "still pained by the retrospect" (28). So while she insists that she has a much better idea than her audience of what slavery means,

she does not hold that her claims to knowledge are themselves complete or unblemished. She also points out that though slaves went through many similar experiences, there is much one slave may not know about the trials of another. For example, Linda Brent rhetorically asks, in connection with another female slave from her hometown: "How could she realize my feelings?" Not having had children herself, Linda implies, Betty couldn't really understand why Linda's attachment to her children made such a difference to her (102; cf. 157).

19. For example, on 201 she does use these images ironically; on 111, she doesn't.

20. Jean Fagan Yellin comments on the variety of ways in which Jacobs uses the "conventions of polite letters" in the "genteel manner of the period" while driving home an unconventional message. See her "Text and Contexts of Harriet Jacobs' Incidents in the Life of a Slave Girl: Written by Herself," in *The Slave's Narrative*, ed. Charles T. Davis and Henry Louis Gates, Jr. (Oxford: Oxford University Press, 1985), especially 267–274. Yellin also points out, in her introduction to *Incidents*, that Jacobs battled against the stereotype of the "tragic mulatto," whose inevitable demise could satisfy the emotions of those whites who prefer their Blacks to come to sad ends rather than achieve freedom (xxx).

21. Though Brent refers to criminal charges against slaves who reveal the names of white men who were fathers of their children (13).

22. Slave women "are considered of no value, unless they continually increase their owner's stock. They are put on a par with animals" (49).

23. Sometimes (180) Linda Brent worries that telling her whole story—"impurities" and all—would risk losing sympathy and the good opinion of someone (in this case Mrs. Bruce).

24. In this connection see Hazel Carby, *Reconstructing Womanhood: The Emergence of the Afro-American Woman Novelist* (New York: Oxford University Press, 1987), 22 and passim.

25. This is not to suggest that pity and compassion are the same.

26. The quotation marks around "race" are meant as a reminder that while the concept has had and continues to have a place in the way we think about ourselves and our histories, there is no good reason to think that the kinds of deep distinctions exist among human beings which the concept typically has been supposed to refer to. An idea doesn't have to be coherent or scientifically well founded in order for it to have profound effects on relationships among human beings. See, for example, Howard Winant and Michael Omi, *Racial Formation in the United States* (New York: Routledge & Kegan Paul, 1986).

27. See Angelina Grimké, letter 7 to Catharine Beecher, in *The Public Years of Sarah and Angelina Grimké: Selected Writings 1835–1839*, ed. Larry Ceplain (New York: Columbia University Press, 1989), passim. (See note 2, chapter 3.)

28. Robin Winks, ed., *Four Fugitive Slave Narratives* (Reading, Mass.: Addison-Wesley, 1969), vi. As quoted in Frances Smith Foster, *Witnessing Slavery: The Development of the Ante-Bellum Slave Narratives* (Westport, Conn.: Greenwood Press, 1979), 20.

29. As quoted by Jean Fagan Yellin in her introduction to *Incidents*, xxii.

30. *Incidents*, 190. At this point in the narrative Linda Brent is describing the importance to her daughter Ellen that her northern school classmates didn't know her slave history: Ellen "had no desire to make capital out of their sympathy."

31. Jacobs does not explicitly refer to the views of contemporary white physicians, such as Samuel A. Cartwright or A. P. Merrill, and others, according to which Blacks were much less sensitive to physical and emotional pain than whites. (On such views, see Martin S. Pernick, *A Calculus of Suffering: Pain, Professionalism, and Anesthesia in Nineteenth-Century America* [New York: Columbia University Press, 1985], 148 ff.) But *Incidents* is liberally sprinkled with her incredulity about whites' incapacity or unwillingness to see the pain around them.

188

For example: "Are doctors of divinity blind, or are they hypocrites? I suppose some are the one, and some the other; but I think if they felt the interest in the poor and lowly, that they ought to feel, they would not get so *easily* blinded" (73, emphasis in original).

32. Another daring aspect of *Incidents* is Jacobs's willingness to express some doubts about the idea that whatever her trials and tribulations on earth, they in no way undermine the existence of a just and powerful God. "Sometimes I thought God was a compassionate Father, who would forgive my sins for the sake of my sufferings. At other times, it seemed to me there was no justice or mercy in the divine government. I asked why the curse of slavery was permitted to exist, and why I had been so persecuted and wronged from youth upward. These things took the shape of mystery, which is to this day not so clear to my soul as I trust it will be hereafter" (123).

33. *OR*, 88–89.

34. Brent, like Frances Harper, surely wishes to be considered as something other than suffering victim; but she doesn't want the facts that make slavery so despicable a condition to be lost sight of.

35. *OR*, 114.

36. The importance of the cognitivist theory of emotions to the possibility of explaining the social and political importance of emotions in our lives will be explored in further detail in chapters 4 and 5.

37. R. W. Hepburn, "The Arts and the Education of Feeling and Emotion," in *Education and Reason*, ed. R. F. Dearden, P. H. Hirst and R. S. Peters (London: Routledge & Kegan Paul, 1972), 94–110.

38. In its various incarnations, this chapter has prompted probing questions and helpful suggestions from Molly Shanley, Uma Narayan, Martha Minow, and patient audiences at Williams College, Miami University, Hartwick College, the Institut für die Wissenschaften vom Menschen in Vienna, and the University of California at Santa Cruz.

Chapter Four

1. Lillian Smith, *Killers of the Dream* (New York: Norton, 1949; 1961), 27.

2. Among such agents, of course, might be the sufferers themselves.

3. See, for example, Eleanor Flexner, *Century of Struggle* (New York: Atheneum, 1972), especially chapter 13; Ellen Carol DuBois, *Feminism and Suffrage* (Ithaca, N.Y.: Cornell University Press, 1978); Angela Davis, *Women, Race, and Class* (New York: Random, 1981); Paula Giddings, *When and Where I Enter: The Impact of Black Women on Race and Sex in America* (New York: Morrow, 1984).

4. In addition to Jacobs's *Incidents in the Life of a Slave Girl*, ed. Jean Fagan Yellin (Cambridge: Harvard University Press, 1987), see Solomon Northrup, *Narrative Solomon Northrup, Twelve Years a Slave*. . . (Auburn, N.Y.: Derby and Miller, 1853) (as quoted in *Black Women in White America*, ed. Gerda Lerner [New York: Vintage, 1972], 51).

5. See, for example, Claudia Koonz, *Mothers in the Fatherland: Women, the Family, and Nazi Politics* (New York: St. Martin's Press, 1987).

6. See, for example, Judith Rollins, *Between Women: Domestics and Their Employers* (Philadelphia: Temple University Press, 1985).

7. This risk is closely related to the one discussed above in chapter 2.

8. See notes 1 through 5 above; and also, for example, bell hooks, *feminist theory: from margin to center* (Boston: South End Press, 1984); Audre Lorde, *Sister Outsider* (Trumansburg, N.Y.: Crossing Press, 1984); Helen E. Longino and Valerie Miner, ed., *Competition: A Feminist Taboo?* (New York: Feminist Press, 1987); Elly Bulkin, Minnie Bruce Pratt, and Barbara Smith, *Yours in Struggle: Feminist Perspectives on Anti-Semitism and Racism* (Ithaca: Firebrand Books, 1984). Simone de Beau-

voir had quite a lot to say about women with race and class privilege undermining or failing to support other women in order to maintain their race and class privilege, but that part of her work is rarely highlighted—even by herself. (See my *Inessential Woman: Problems of Exclusion in Feminist Thought* [Boston: Beacon Press, 1988], chapter 3.)

9. Berenice Fisher, "Guilt and Shame in the Women's Movement: The Radical Ideal of Action and Its Meaning for Feminist Intellectuals," *Feminist Studies* 10, no. 2 (Summer 1984): 186.

10. See Carol Gilligan, *In a Different Voice: Psychological Theory and Women's Development* (Cambridge: Harvard University Press, 1982); Nel Noddings, *Caring: A Feminine Approach to Ethics and Moral Education* (Berkeley: University of California Press, 1984); *Women and Moral Theory*, ed. Eva Feder Kittay and Diana T. Meyers (Savage, Md.: Rowman and Littlefield, 1987).

11. Jane Austen, *Emma* (New York: Bantam, 1981; originally published, 1816), 133–139.

12. These are not incompatible conceptions, according to Gilligan and others. See *Women and Moral Theory*, op. cit.

13. See, for example, *Women and Moral Theory* (op. cit.); Lawrence A. Blum, "Gilligan and Kohlberg: Implications for Moral Theory," *Ethics* 98 (April 1988): 472–491.

14. *Emma*, 139–140.

15. Judith Rollins, *Between Women: Domestics and Their Employers* (Philadelphia: Temple University Press, 1985), 186.

16. Two problems emerge here, even in the presentation of (1)–(4): one is what it means for institutions, as opposed to individuals, to have such reactions; and the other is that as long as we focus on institutions, we don't have to think about what our own reactions are.

17. Gabriele Taylor, *Pride, Shame, and Guilt: Emotions of Self-Assessment* (Oxford: Clarendon Press, 1985).

18. See my "Anger and Insubordination," in *Women, Knowledge, and Reality*, ed. Ann Garry and Marilyn Pearsall (Winchester, Mass.: Unwin and Hyman, 1989), 263–273.

19. While regretting that something happened differs in some important ways from regretting having done something—since the latter, not the former, entails responsibility for having done the act in question—I can fully regret that an event happened without in any way implicating myself in having brought it about.

20. In "Cognitive Emotions?" Chesire Calhoun discusses the repair work necessary for certain versions of the cognitive theory in light of the fact that sometimes "one's doxic life and one's emotional life part company" (in *What Is an Emotion? Classic Readings in Philosophical Psychology*, ed. Chesire Calhoun and Robert C. Solomon [New York: Oxford University Press, 1984], 333).

21. Notice how odd it would be to refer to that about which one feels shame as merely an "incident."

22. See my *Inessential Woman*.

23. Thanks to Claudia Card for sound editorial advice.

Chapter Five

1. As quoted in Jean Fagan Yellin, *Women and Sisters: The Antislavery Feminists in American Culture* (New Haven: Yale University Press, 1989), 171.

2. Yellin, 60.

3. Martin Pernick, *A Calculus of Suffering: Pain, Professionalism, and Anesthesia in Nineteenth-Century America* (New York: Columbia University Press, 1985).

4. Yellin, 44.

5. Yellin, 29, 43.

6. Yellin, 30, 39, 43.

7. Yellin, 30.

8. Yellin describes a later development in this gradual "universalizing" of the situation of Black slaves in the work of the sculptor Hiram Powers. Powers's "The Greek Slave" (1841–1843), according to Yellin "the most popular American sculpture of the nineteenth century" (100), depicted an erect, bare-breasted woman with "caucasian" features; though like the Black female slave still chained, this figure shows no sign of resistance. On the contrary, Yellin suggests, a small but unmistakable cross bespeaks Christian resignation to the fact of suffering. Many contemporary observers, Yellin reports, took this sculpted slave's plight to be representative of the human condition, an "emblem of all trial to which humanity is subject" (107).

9. bell hooks, *feminist theory: from margin to center* (Boston: South End Press, 1984), 5–6.

10. Harriet A. Jacobs, *Incidents in the Life of a Slave Girl, Written by Herself*, ed. Jean Fagan Yellin (Cambridge: Harvard University Press, 1987). See chapter 3.

11. June Jordan, "Report from the Bahamas," in *On Call* (Boston: South End Press, 1985), 43.

12. "Playfulness, 'World'-Traveling, and Loving Perception," in *Women, Knowledge, and Reality: Explorations in Feminist Philosophy*, ed. Ann Garry and Marilyn Pearsall (Boston: Unwin Hyman, 1989), 279.

13. Cf. Renato Rosaldo: "The modest truism that any human groups must have certain things in common can appear to fly in the face of a once-healthy methodological caution that warns against the reckless attribution of one's own categories and experiences to members of another culture. Such warnings against facile notions of universal human nature can be carried too far and harden into the equally pernicious doctrine that, my own group aside, everything human is alien to me." "Grief and a headhunter's rage: On the cultural force of emotions," in *Play, Text, and Story*, ed. Edward Bruner (Proceedings of the 1983 Meeting of the American Ethnological Society, Washington, D.C.), 188.

14. In another sense we make ourselves their bellhops: we carry the baggage of their experience and make it look as if it is our own.

15. Several claims come to mind, some of them more justifiable than others. There is the claim that unless you actually have gone through what I've gone through, you can't understand what I mean when I talk about it; then the somewhat weaker claim that unless you could go through the kind of experience I've gone through, you can't understand what I mean when I talk about it; then the even weaker claim that unless you know the kinds of circumstances that would verify or at least warrant what I say, or correlatively the kinds of circumstances that would falsify or at least throw into doubt the truth of what I say, you can't understand what I mean when I talk about an experience I have undergone (so even if you haven't had, and even if you couldn't have, the experiences I've had, as someone who shares the language in which I speak you nevertheless can know what I mean). Philosophers influenced by Wittgenstein are likely to balk at the first two claims, insisting that the price any of us pays for the opportunity to speak meaningfully about her or his own experience is the concession that anyone else can, in principle, understand such an experience, and the recognition that others might also have such an experience. Such philosophers accept as a fact no longer in need of explanation that "the idea of experience is the idea of states and events of sorts which can be enjoyed by others" (Christopher Peacocke, "Consciousness and Other Minds (1)" [*Proceedings of the Aristotelian Society*, supplementary vol. 58 (1984), 105]). On such an understanding of experience, there is no such thing as an experience only one person can have;

even if not everyone can have a given experience (childbirth), that hardly means *only* one person could possibly have it.

16. Lawrence Blum, "Compassion," in *Explaining Emotions*, ed. Amélie Oksenberg Rorty (Berkeley: University of California Press, 1980), 511. A slightly revised version appears in his *Moral Perception and Particularity* (New York: Cambridge University Press, 1994), 173–182.

17. Blum, 510, 511.

18. Blum, 512.

19. If Blum identifies a moral failure in pity as the refusal to regard oneself as a possible subject of the undesirable experience, the example from June Jordan referred to above suggests a moral failure in a certain kind of envy as the refusal to regard oneself as a possible subject in an allegedly desirable experience. Although it is perhaps even more complicated than that, since Jordan's account suggests that the white women's envy may in fact be a disguised form of pity.

20. Trans. Alexander Nehamas and Paul Woodruff (Indianapolis: Hackett, 1989).

21. See chapter 2.

22. T. H. Irwin, "Generosity and Property in Aristotle's *Politics*," in *Beneficence, Philanthropy and the Public Good*, ed. Ellen Frankel Paul, Fred D. Miller, Jr., Jeffrey Paul, and John Ahrens (Oxford: Blackwell, 1987), 49–50.

23. Indeed, different kinds of pleasurable experiences are to be had by different kinds of people. There are modes of music better suited to please "artisans, laborers, and the like," whose "minds are perverted from their natural state," than are suited to the quite different experiences of pleasure known by the "free and educated" (*Politics* 1342a19–22).

24. *New Yorker*, 8 Apr. 1991, 73, advertisement, top-right corner.

25. Toni Morrison, "Unspeakable Things Unspoken: The Afro-American Presence in American Literature," *Michigan Quarterly Review* 27, no. 1 (Winter 1989): 6.

26. Yellin, 23–25.

27. Morrison, 10.

28. *Boston Globe*, Saturday, 15 Sept. 1990, p. 22.

29. Hayden Herrera, "Why Frida Kahlo Speaks to the 90's," *New York Times*, Sunday, 28 Oct. 1990, sec. 2, p. 41.

30. Mary Helen Washington, editor's introduction, *Invented Lives: Narratives of Black Women 1860–1960* (Garden City, N.Y.: Anchor-Doubleday, 1987), xix.

31. Washington, 3, 10.

32. See Yellin, passim, for a discussion of the portrayal of the Black female slave as in "speechless agony."

33. Lucy S. Dawidowicz, "Thinking about the Six Million: Facts, Figures, Perspectives," in *Holocaust: Religious and Philosophical Implications*, ed. John K. Roth and Michael Berenbaum (New York: Paragon House, 1989), 63.

34. Dawidowicz, 63.

35. Karl Morrison, *"I Am You": The Hermeneutics of Empathy in Western Literature, Theology, and Art* (Princeton: Princeton University Press, 1988).

36. Morrison, 7.

37. Morrison, xxv; cf. 82.

38. Morrison, 30, 60, xxvi.

39. Morrison, 81, 236. These worries about empathy did not seem to occur to Hannah Arendt. See chapter 3.

40. Morrison does not conclude, of course, that all cases of empathy involve domination. In this connection it might be instructive to try to unpack what was meant by the unnamed Black woman from Harlem reported to have said of Nelson Mandela: "He is us and we are him" (*Nation*, 16 July 1990, 77).

41. For thoughtful and incisive comments on earlier drafts, I am grateful to Martha Minow, Nalini Bhushan, Pamela Hall, and audiences at the University of Virginia, Kenyon College, Union College, Boston University, Georgia State University, University of Pittsburgh, Suffolk University, Harvard Divinity School, University of Wisconsin at Madison, and Dalhousie University.

Chapter Six

1. Arlene Croce, "Discussing the Undiscussable," *New Yorker*, 24 Dec. 1994/ 2 Jan. 1995, 54–60. Page references in the text are to this article.

2. Croce seems to assume that most of the dancing itself is done by people who are very ill. Jones has said that he explicitly chose to use "a youthful, healthy group of dancers" and that they would not be trying to "impersonate the sick and dying" (*Last Night on Earth*, by Bill T. Jones with Peggy Gillespie [New York: Pantheon, 1995], 263 and 252). Reviews by critics who actually saw the performance—see, for example, Lynn Garafola, note 4—presuppose a distinction between the dancers and those whose stories about illness are seen on videos. Croce is right: she didn't need to see the dance to say what she had to say. But to many who actually saw the dance, she in fact needed *not* to see the dance to say what she had to say.

3. Obviously Croce did not intend to write a philosophical treatise on the proper relation between suffering and art. By calling this credo "Crocean" I mean to suggest that while Croce did not explicitly create the following recipe, she certainly contributed a lot of the ingredients. So "Crocean Stew" might be a better rubric.

4. Lynn Garafola, "Black Dance: Revelations," *Nation*, 17 Apr. 1995, 537.

5. See Terry Teachout, "Victim Art," *Commentary*, March 1995, 58–61, for a review of such responses.

6. As quoted by John Leo, "The backlash against victim art," *U.S. News & World Report*, 16 Jan. 1995, 22.

7. Vicki Goldberg, "Looking at the Poor in a Gilded Frame," *New York Times*, Sunday, 9 Apr. 1995, sec. 2, pp. 1, 39.

8. Elizabeth Prelinger, "Kollwitz Reconsidered," in *Käthe Kollwitz*, by Elizabeth Prelinger with essays by Alessandra Comini and Hildegard Bachert (Washington: National Gallery of Art, and New Haven: Yale University Press, 1992), 79.

9. Of course, a work of art doesn't have to mean anything. However, there may be unclarity about whether it is appropriate to look for "meaning": "Mark Rothko claimed . . . that if the spectator read his paintings solely in terms of spatial and color relationships, then he had failed to understand them. 'You might as well get one thing straight,' he once told an interviewer. 'I'm not an abstractionist. . . . I'm not interested in the relationship of color or form to anything else. I'm interested in expressing basic human emotions. . . . And the fact that a lot of people break down and cry when confronted with my pictures shows . . . they are having the same religious experience I had when I painted them.'" Suzi Gablik, *Has Modernism Failed?* (New York: Thames and Hudson, 1984), 22.

10. *Art in America*, March 1996, 92.

11. Compare this to Croce's worries about another kind of deal (see #6 above): you put sufferers on stage, I'll feel sorry for them, and we'll all call it art.

12. David Carroll, foreword to Jean-François Lyotard, *Heidegger and "the Jews"* (Minneapolis, 1990), 11. As quoted in Saul Friedlander, "Introduction," *Probing the Limits of Representation: Nazism and the "Final Solution"* (Cambridge: Harvard University Press, 1992), 6.

13. Michael R. Marrus, "The Use and Misuse of the Holocaust," *Lessons and Legacies: The Meaning of the Holocaust in a Changing World*, ed. Peter Hayes (Evanston: Northwestern University Press, 1991), 107.

14. Ibid.

15. See Alvin Rosenfeld, "The Holocaust according to William Styron," *Midstream*, December 1979, 49. As quoted by Marrus; see note 13.

Conclusion

1. The profiteer certainly counts on the presence of a generally shared perception that the loss is serious or the suffering undesirable, in order for the images of the suffering to draw attention to prospective consumers.

2. See, for example, Joan Tronto, *Moral Boundaries: A Political Argument for an Ethic of Care* (New York: Routledge, 1993).

Index

Index

Index